In reference to Rowing Tales 2019

"It was such a delight to read the varied stories of rowing enthusiasts. We all come to rowing from different paths, but once there, we are immediately, instantly, family. Each story was relatable and inspiring. That is a good thing for those of us preparing for the long 5 months of indoor winter training. Such history in these stories as well. I learned different perspectives to the "Boys in the Boat" story, the history of the Head of the Charles, and the Royal Henley's many rivalries. It was also super fun to read 3 stories from women that row in my own club!"

Nancy Mack
Masters Rower and Coach
Any Boat, Any Seat, Anywhere, Anytime

"Rowing is very much like life and the friendships you make. Having worked with the lovely Andrew Probert for five years, I left for New Zealand and kept in touch via Facebook. By accident, I befriended his friend Rebecca, who edits Rowing Tales. I expected the book to be out of reach for a humble spectator and one-season novice rower. How wrong I was! The stories from amateur adult rowers reflect mine. It's a treasure trove."

Jade Badcock
A technical author in the New Zealand public service, rowing fan and an awful rower.

"Reading Rowing Tales is like going to a family reunion - aunts and uncles, parents and siblings sharing incredible stories over beers and laughter. Some funny, some inspiring, all of them important, as part of the history we - the members of the rowing clan - share. And all of them inspiring us to get back on the water or keep our hand in the game, so we can write brilliant stories of our own. Read it to remember why you row."

Charles Sweeney
Masters Rower

A Haiku for Rowing

"Rowing Tales 2018?
Magnificent Memories,
Beyond the Rainbow!"

Martha DeLong
Old Lady Rower

"Rowing Tales is a collection of anecdotes from all over the world ranging across a whole variety of topics - nature, physics, self healing - and from learn to rowers to Olympic champions. You may, like me, have relatives and friends who wonder about your strange obsession; this would be a good book to give them which might help explain it."

Christopher Anton
Cox, rowing administrator, regional chair, NGB
member and FISA umpire

Rowing Tales

Rebecca Caroe

Rowing Tales

Copyright 2019 by Rebecca Caroe

All rights reserved. No part of this publication may be reproduced or transmitted in any form by any means, electronic or mechanical, including photocopy, or any information storage or retrieval system, without written permission of the publisher, except in cases of brief quotation by reviewers or commentators. Printed in the UK.

First Printing: October 2019

Dedication

To my husband, Grant, whose unfailing support and tolerance for
my crazy rowing projects gives me fortitude.
I can't do it without you.

From the Editor

Rowing Tales has become an annual publication. Since the first edition in 2017 when I thought this might be a one-off, I have now realised that there is a gigantic resource of stories waiting to be told.

Our sport creates passion in its participants, supporters and coaches. Sometimes I puzzle about why this is so particular and somewhat different from other sports. I've thought that it might be because of teamwork in the boat, or shared community while endlessly rigging and de-rigging boats at regattas, or maybe the toughening effect of hard training done with crew mates. All these reasons seem insufficient to explain the intensity of emotion which comes from the sport of rowing.

Now I believe that part of our passion comes from telling and re-telling rowing stories.

And so to all who have gone before us, to the current generation of rowers and to all who will come after us - keep telling your rowing tales. Whether told straight-up or embellished to create more drama, I don't mind. What I enjoy is the rush of feelings which I get while listening to your rowing stories.

And so, please enjoy this book. Leave it by your bed, in the bathroom, in the boathouse. Let others dip in and read; send a copy to an old rowing friend.

Spellings for US and British English are used interchangeably depending on the nationality of the author.

Above all, keep rowing, keep coaching, keep coxing, keep recruiting and keep supporting our wonderful sport.

Rebecca Caroe,
Auckland, New Zealand
1 October 2019

Introduction

The RowingChat podcast network is one of my principal sources of great rowing stories. I started broadcasting in 2013 doing interviews with coaches and athletes and found in the course of these leisurely chats that people are incredibly generous with their time, their insights and knowledge. The stories just seem to fall out of a broader discussion on rowing.

During 2018 I decided to expand the podcast into a network of rowing-related podcasts and this has had the delightful side-effect of surfacing even more rowing stories. My co-hosts of the many different shows have been fantastic detectives helping to interview so many folks and encourage them to tell their stories live on air.

There is room for many more voices in the network. We welcome new perspectives. Do join us as a listener or a host.

https://rowing.chat/

Authors

Chris Brake	1
Morgan Hellen	2
David Calder	4
Ted Nash	5
William de Laszlo	7
Emma Shaw	9
Stacie Giddings	11
Jackie Quinlan-Dorbeck	16
Jim Dietz	22
Charlotte Pierce	23
Tidying The Tideway	25
Noel Donaldson	27
Caroline Buckley	29
Alan Campbell	31
Bryan Kitch	33
Chris Madell	34
Gloria DiFulvio	37
Michael d'Eredita	40
Martin Cross	43
Aly Mielbrandt and Tonia Williams	45
Bill Mitchell	47
Anonymous	48
Judy Rantz Williams	53

Gloria DiFulvio	69
Lawrence Fogelberg	71
Rebecca Caroe	94
Greg Spooner	97
William de Laszlo	99
Peter Becker	101
Bryan Volpenhein	103
Noel Donaldson	105
The Washington Post	108
Northeastern University	110
CeCe Aguda	113
Wendy "Pepper" Schuss	117
Chris Madell	120

Chris Brake

Every rowing coach has a nuanced relationship with their athletes. Coaching adults brings out a range of different actions and reactions from both parties. Many coaches know their charges better than their parents because they see each other daily and coach in situations of extreme stress which brings out details of their characters which are not often seen.

Chris is the father of Michael Brake, stroke of the New Zealand pair whose image is on the front cover of this book. While we were having breakfast after a weekend outing, Chris told this story to the mother of the athlete in question.

Megaphone Malfunction

I was out coaching the squad in the upper harbour. There were a group of athletes all in singles and when we got to the turn around point, one of the girls manoeuvered her boat close to the coaching launch.

She started explaining all sorts of spurious stuff about the row, about her poor technique, about her bad state of mind and generally complaining about her rowing.

I picked up my megaphone and started tapping the side of it; holding it to my ear and then tapping it again with a puzzled look on my face.

"What are you doing?" the athlete asked.

"I'm checking my megaphone, it has a whining sound coming out of it! I hope it'll go away." I replied.

She sculled off.

Morgan Hellen

A former British international athlete, Morgan is busy launching a rowing business, Rowith, an app to allow rowers to get guided audio workouts to row together on the indoor rowing machine.

Mum, I Don't Want To Go

I started rowing when I was 11 with the local after-school rowing club. I went to Oakwood Park Grammar School in Kent, UK. It was just an indoor rowing club and happened every Monday afternoon. It was run by John Clayton who founded Maidstone Rowing Club which is the local rowing club where I grew up.

Initially, I was doing dry-rowing and since I was bigger than the average 11-year-old it gave me a bit of an advantage on the rowing machine. John invited me down to the local rowing club to try water rowing where I joined the junior team. I spent a few years there.

Around the age of 14, I was also playing rugby. I was really involved in the rugby team. I was kind of weighing up whether I wanted to follow rowing or play rugby.

It was a Saturday morning which is one of the days when the junior rowing team trains at Maidstone. I woke up and I thought, "Oh, I don't think I really want to go. I'd rather play rugby tomorrow – on Sunday. I'm just not feeling up for it."

I told my Mum, "I don't want to go." She said, "Well, I'm not telling the coach. You tell him yourself." What I did was I emailed the coach. "Hi Ray. I'm not going to make it to training today." He wrote back to me. "See you on Wednesday."

At that time, I wasn't going rowing on Wednesdays because I had rugby training on Wednesdays.

I thought to myself, "Well now, I can't not go on Wednesday because he said, 'See you on Wednesday. 'So, I missed rugby training; I went to Wednesday rowing."

I just fell in love with it and decided, "Rugby is done. Let's stick with the rowing."

From there, I carried on rowing and got better. I ended up training five, six times a week. I went to the Junior World Rowing Championships. I went to the Coupe de la Jeunesse which is a European championships for juniors. And this led to a scholarship to study at the University of California Berkeley in the United States and eventually the British Rowing team.

It all started with not wanting to go rowing on a Saturday morning.

David Calder

Dave Calder is a Canadian international rower and veteran of four Olympic Games from 2000 - 2012. He won silver in the pair at the Beijing 2008 Olympic Games and is now the Executive Director of Rowing British Columbia, Canada.

Rowing Fast As Lightning

Each year at our training camp in Erba (northern Italy) we have at least one big storm, which usually includes lightning. It's welcomed though because the accompanying rain cools and clears the air, which is usually a humid 36 degrees Celsius (86 degrees Farenheit).

Coming from the west coast of Canada, I can count on one hand the number of times I've been faced with lightning there while rowing. The one that stands out most in my memory happened in Seattle.

It was my freshman year at UW (University of Washington, USA) and the legendary John Parker was my coach. We were about a kilometer from the boathouse, at the finish-line end of the Montlake Cut, when a storm rolled in. John saw the first flash of lightning and hit the throttle of his wakeless launch. Only as an afterthought did he yell back at us over his megaphone "Take the boats back to the Conni."

His fear of lightning endeared him to us, because that was the first sign of emotion he'd shown us all year that wasn't perfectly calculated.

Later that year when we painted our class motto on the side of The Cut we remembered John and that stormy day, painting "Every move is like lightning".

Ted Nash

I find Rowing Tales in some very unlikely places. This one came from an anonymous source on the RSR discussion newsgroup. Ted Nash is a rower and coach who represented the USA at the Rome (1960) and Tokyo (1964) Olympic Games winning a gold and bronze medal before taking up coaching at University of Pennsylvania and US Rowing.

Coach Controls The Weather

We all know that Ted Nash actually controls the weather and here is a story demonstrating that truism.

A couple summers ago we were preparing for the World Championships and as we showed up for our evening practice the rain was really coming down. Lightning was cracking every few moments. Ted is famous for being immune to the weather conditions and told us to warm up to the top (about 3 miles) and meet him there.

I thought he was kidding, but the PACRA vets told me he was very serious. We were the only crews on the river as the electrical storm was becoming pretty fierce. Ted said that the weather would cooperate by the time we got to the top, and that would give us a three mile lead on the Romulans (his name for the Romanians who were our arch rivals).

Well the rain and lightning got much worse. It was really dark and downpouring and flashes of lightning every few seconds. Now for people who don't know Ted, he is quite a presence. He has a deep booming voice. He doesn't need a megaphone, but uses one anyway making his coaching commands sound like they are coming down from Mount Olympus or Valhalla. Anyway, we were supposed to be doing some 2k pieces at "96% intensity", but because of the weather we were going to do some 4.5 minute pieces on the way home.

Ted has an unusual way to start the pieces, instead of "On this one!" or "Ready all...ROW!" etc, Ted says "We're breathing, we're breathing, And...AWAY....WE....GO!!!" which was always confusing to me as some of the guys would go on "Away" and some on "We" and I was waiting for "GO!!!!" (The motto of most Philly guys is "If you ain't cheatin, you ain't tryin'.).

Well we were trying to get back to the dock as fast as possible so Ted was abbreviating his start commands. He was starting us by relative speed so we would all be close at the end of the pieces. "Light women's single.....GO!!!" pause "Women's Double.....GO!!" pause "Women's four.....GO!!!!" pause.

Then it was just us and I was looking right at him as he said "Men's pair......HAAAAAAHHHH!!!" and as he yelled it he punched the air above him and made a fist, and at that exact moment a bolt of lightning struck the shore behind him making a deafening CRACK!!!

This was about the most memorable rowing experience I have ever experienced – the day Ted Nash threw lightning bolts at me.

William de Laszlo

William de Laszlo is an ocean rower whose crew set the Guinness World Record in 2005 for rowing around the United Kingdom coastline. He continues to run the GB Row Challenge race which replicates that course.

In this Rowing Tale from his record-setting row he shares a moment of clarity into the fragility of his own life, while facing peril during a tempest.

Compare this to the Unhurried Moment tale later in the book and see the similarities where both authors describe how time moves into a different pace, almost dream-like and definitely not at the same pace as time normally passes. I think rowing often creates an "other-worldliness" for us participants. We just have to be sufficiently mindful and present in the moment to recognise its presence.

Storm At Sea

We set out to get into the Guinness Book of Records as the fastest row around United Kingdom mainland.

Our route was not decided in advance because we could cut through inside islands and what-have-you.

I suppose there are a number of decision points that we had to make. For example, at Land's End, do we go straight out into the Irish Sea? Do we try and stick close to the coast and use the cover of Ireland on the inside, so you are kind of tracking up the inside of Ireland? Or would you just, as I said, go straight down the middle?

In particular, I remember having quite an intense conversation with the crew – because I was the skipper of the boat – saying that there would be forecast gale force winds going into the Irish Sea. Actually, our plan was to use Ireland to provide us cover, but we never got across to Ireland, so we were stuck out in the middle of the Irish Sea in one of the most extraordinary storms I've ever been in.

It was terrifying to a degree. Luckily, the wind was behind us, so it was pushing us up the Irish Sea, but it was one of those moments that I'll never forget.

It's sending shivers down my spine even thinking about it.

As we got out into the storm, weather conditions were building. Wind was building and boat speed was building with the wind behind us, increasing the size of the waves to a point where we were starting to surf down the front of the waves.

Now, for anybody who surfs, that's great if you're going down a wave, but what generally happens is your boat starts to turn to the left or to the right. If that happened, then our boat would have rolled down the face of the wave.

We paid out something like 200 metres of rope. We had our sea anchor out to really try and hold us back, so our boat was being pulled through the waves to slow our descent.

I'll never forget this one moment when we were in the middle of the storm. It's kind of chaos, but we're continuing to row because you had to stay on deck the whole time. We were all latched and strapped in.

I'll never forget these seagulls just playing in the water – probably about 25 metres away from us. As the waves were so big, they were in this kind of stillness of almost a pocket of air, and they were just mucking around. I just remember thinking to myself, "We're so vulnerable. We're so small in this huge ocean."

It was one of those real moments where you think, "Crikey! I could be fish food in the next 30 minutes," and these birds wouldn't care, and life goes on.

It's really exhilarating. We got out the other side of it fine, but it was quite an extraordinary experience.

Emma Shaw

Emma Shaw was a promising tennis player who discovered rowing during a summer at Windridge Tennis Camp, just down the road from the Craftsbury Sculling Centre, Vermont, USA. She explains "I came home from tennis camp and told my bemused parents about what it felt like to scull". Before her junior year, she returned to Craftsbury, this time as 'glorified grunt', in exchange for instruction and time on the lake returning to school eager to fill her long-time goal of rowing in addition to coxing. The coaches were kind enough to let her race a scull for the final two years at university while coxing a sweep crew. She rowed and coxed for the University of North Carolina at Chapel Hill, USA and the University of St Andrews, Scotland where this story is set.

One Stroke Decision: Why Did I Choose Rowing?

Don't you sometimes wonder why you row? Why did you start and is it worth it to go through all the pain and unpleasant training?

Some days ago, I again questioned my decision to row. Not my previous experiences, or the likelihood that future conversations will be centered on the effect rowing has had on my life. Simply, my decision to continue to row for this very practice.

I'm standing in a beautiful place; a sailing club overlooking a long, winding stretch of the River Tay. Behind me are mountains underlined by an orange stripe of trees. Beyond the river, are lush green fields with white-roaming specks, the ever-present sheep wearing much warmer kit than my teammates and I.

Perth, Scotland is a beautiful place, and yet all I can focus on is my feet.

Cold and wet, standing barefoot in the grass, this feeling is only the beginning. I'm in short tights, because soon we have to wade into the piercing cold waters, down a steep and muddy incline. If I wear long tights, they'll be completely submerged when my 5'1" frame inevitably meets the water more than halfway up my legs; a problem of the perpetual bowman, perhaps. Once we place our boat on the surface, I'll either stand in the water, undoing gates to take my mind off the watery needles inserting themselves into my legs, or I'll emerge to grab bow pair's oars, jabbing my cold feet into the sharp edges of an uneven concrete slipway. After it's done, we'll stand in the water until the middle pairs get in the boat, until finally, finally, we're asked to join our crewmates in the shell. Next, our coxswain will ask us – the bow pair – to take strokes away from the shore, silently acknowledging our delayed gratification of warm socks in her request.

My one stroke decision.

Before I can dread what's next any longer, internally bemoaning the extra seconds I'll spend with my feet bare in the cold water as we help guide the boat to the middle of the river, I break my reverie to place my blade in the water. In those brief moments that we rowers spend so much time practicing, I press my handle down and let my hands lead my body toward the catch. A simple release of the handle and the blade drops into the water and I move back to where I started. The cold and wetness is an afterthought and the dread of the inevitable cold of practice falls away.

It only ever takes one stroke to assuage my doubts.

Why do I still row? There are more reasons than single strokes, even if the answer can be found in every single stroke. But for now: because I love it, because it makes me face my doubts, and because anything less enjoyable than a single stroke simply washes away before the puddle fades.

Not a one stroke decision.

Stacie Giddings

Stacie lives in Northampton, MA, USA and has been rowing with the Northampton Community Rowing Club for the entirety of her 3 year career. Stacie and her friends enjoy rowing with other clubs around the state and country (and for some of them, the world), and they recently started building a fleet of their own. Stacie loves rowing adventures and getting into the flow while rowing hard, fast, and with purpose with her crew.

Rowing Is A Journey, Not A Destination

The evening is waning. I am with my crewmates, at first battling the motorboats and jet skis as they create a wake that irritates. We soon forget about the disruption, as we watch a heron strut along the banks of the Connecticut River, and wave at Charly the bald eagle as he tends to his nest of young eaglets. As we approach the yellow house on the Hadley side of river, we are in awe we've made it here so quickly. It's time to turn around. Our focus shifts from drills and nature to rowing. Eight bodies contracting, reaching, pushing, pulling; eight oar handles turning in unison. We glide over the water. We are in the zone, rowing as one. Catch, drive, swish, release; catch, drive, swish, release.

The sun is setting. It is beautiful, and I am at peace.

Before to moving to Northampton, I was like a ship lost at sea. The light from my lighthouse was too dim to guide my path. Over the ten years prior to moving here, I'd divorced the father of my children and started a successful career. I ended a second relationship that wasn't ideal for me, yet as in my marriage, I'd stayed for years longer than I should have. Then came the man I thought was my perfect match - my partner in crime, the peanut to my butter, the grape to my jelly, and we married. I allowed myself to become absorbed into his life, as I had in past relationships, because it was easier to lose myself in someone else's world than to focus on my own. Besides, he was fun and the life of the party. He lived on a lake and had a boat. Who doesn't want that? Turns out, me.

Why did this long-time bachelor only want to link boats, drink rum and float Lake Minnetonka in the summer; followed by drinking rum and playing hockey on Lake Minnetonka in the winter? At first it was good enough for me too, but I rebelled. "Let's take a drive to Wisconsin and look at the fall leaves," I'd say. "We can do that here," he'd say. I said, "Let's go to Duluth for the weekend." He said, "I've been there."

He was confused I was no longer content orbiting his life. I was angry he didn't want to incorporate my individuality into his world. Isn't it ironic? I expected him to know what I wanted when I didn't know myself?

The marriage soon dissolved, and I was sad, distraught, and lost. I'd left my job, where I was burning my candle at both ends, to live the lake life with the man of my dreams; the man who'd saved me, and now I was alone. Really alone.

The professionals I was paying to help me suggested I turn the spotlight on myself instead of focusing on all the ways he'd wronged me. I learned from the great teacher, hindsight, that my second failed marriage was a blessing in disguise and a catalyst to my own healing. As I forced myself to look in the mirror, I quickly discovered I was seeking someone to fill my voids. To provide me with security, strength and confidence. Now without the compass of another, I didn't know what to do. I couldn't identify what made me tick, and it was frightening. How did this happen to me? How did I get here?

My closest friends and family would be surprised by this confession. As a child, I was a super confident, look at me, I'm an amazing and adventurous kind of kid. I was the one who protected the bullied on the playground and did not hesitate to call out the aggressors. I didn't care what people thought of me. Looking back on it, I recognize my parents didn't know what to do with me. They were both so young when they had me, and I was way more questioning and rebellious than anyone else in the family. But I was not strong enough to overcome my life experiences, and I succumbed to the pressure to conform. I used to boast that I could change colors and blend in to any surrounding, fit in with any personality or relationship. I needed to feel loved and accepted by everyone, and this made it easier. But being a chameleon came with a price. I lost my true nature and intuition, and no longer knew who I was.

After my second divorce, I didn't know what to do. I couldn't organize myself around my family because my kids were grown and on their own, my sisters lived in separate states, I didn't want to move back to Nebraska, and I definitely didn't take root in Minnesota. I was alone, for the first time in my life. I could literally go anywhere, or nowhere. When I was offered a job in Northampton, I wasn't running away as much as I was seeking and accepting what came. I've lived a lot of places, but I'd never so much as visited Massachusetts, let alone New England, and with the exception of New York City, the Northeast. While I've always organized my life around other people's passions, I've never lost my adventurous spirit. Now my dim guiding light was leading me to Western Mass, where I'd have no one to blame but me for not considering me and my life.

My first week in Northampton I walked by a group of fundraisers rowing ergs on the courthouse lawn. This sight must have lit a fire because completely out of the passive character I'd become, I sought out a rowing club like a woman possessed.

Fortunately, I didn't have to look far - the rowers on the green were Northampton Community Rowers. I relentlessly tracked down the coach and peppered him with questions. That one 'learn to row 'class I took three years prior qualified me to be an Intermediate rower as far as this coach was concerned. Sure, that experience had been on the Mighty Mississippi River, but because of heavy flooding, it was too dangerous to take out anything but a training barge that year. I was very clear about this, but the coach assured me he'd give me a quick refresher. I was skeptical, but ready to jump right in.

I showed up for day one. I'd never carried a boat. All the commands were foreign to me. Weigh enough? What? Thank god I was good at following. Now I'm sitting in the boat...with seven other people. Err, make that eight. What is a coxswain? What number is my seat? I was familiar with port and starboard from our boat on Lake Minnetonka, but it was all backwards now that the bow was behind me. And what the heck is an oar lock? Feather what? Square huh? I could not recall any of these terms from my Minnesota coursework, yet here I was, sitting in this long narrow vessel with eight people, and this people pleaser did not want to disappoint!

My crewmates were kind, accepting, and patient with me. "Push your oar against the oar lock," they'd say as I struggled to gain control of my body. They followed up with a "great job," when I got it right. I was not kind, accepting or patient with myself, "How can you be in this boat when you don't even know this basic thing?" my inner voice would say.

On day two, even worse, we had a coach with an Eastern European accent, and she kept yelling at me (she called it coaching). "Three seat!" She yelled for what felt like the billionth time. "Vatch your catch timing! You aren't leesening to me!" "I am listening to you... I'm just three commands behind you trying to remember what catch means!" Did I see her smile behind that bullhorn or was it a grimace? It didn't matter. I went home and watched rowing videos and studied the mechanics of boat dynamics in my spare time, and soon enough, I was pulling my own weight.

When I'm in the boat, giving it my all, I lose track of time and space. I love that I'm out in nature, but I forget that's where I am. I am doing my individual best for the good of my crewmates. I watch the boat glide over the water with the guidance of our collective oars and coxswain. The more focused and synchronised we are, the smoother our ride. Rowing is teaching me a lot about life. If my stroke isn't perfect, I'm much kinder to myself.

Like life, rowing is a journey, not a destination, and I am finding myself.

I came to Northafmpton alone and lost. In a few summer evenings, I had found a family in these rowers; a community of love and support. This magical place is full of diversity and acceptance. I am convinced a divine source led me to Northampton, and rowing. While still a work in progress, I see my life more clearly. My light is shining more brightly. It led me here. I am finding my way. I understand - truly understand - gratitude now. I experience it in almost everything I do. I am living more in the moment and less in the memories and mistakes of the past, less in my head worrying what the future holds for me. I am in my boat, with my crew, in this moment- working together with love, and grace, and acceptance, and forgiveness.

I am home. Catch, drive, swish, release. Release. Release.

Jackie Quinlan-Dorbeck

As this story explains, Jackie began her own rowing in the past year. She lives in Auckland, New Zealand.

The Beginning Of My Rowing Journey

I have followed my children's rowing for a good number of years now. Five of my six children rowed and I have loved supporting them throughout their many years of commitment to the sport. The last few seasons I worked alongside my husband in the boat park as a member of the maintenance team. I also created a role as parent-support for coxswains when many of the Westlake Boys High School coxswains were leaving the sport. The rowing boys had to take turns to squeeze their large bodies into the small coxswain seat and cox the training sessions one winter. After my son's time with rowing I know the rowing boys pretty well and I feel that I belong, I have a place with Westlake rowing.

Last season was my youngest child's last year of schoolboy rowing. I was feeling a sense of relief but also grief at this big part of my life being taken away. One of the Westlake girls who had left school the year before and was still rowing told me that it is great to have had parents 'support at school level but that it is now so fun to be on their own as young adult rowers. So, where would rowing be in my life now? In the past only? It was all something that I had yet to confront but was heading toward rapidly.

The end was coming.

Until the day Fiona (another rowing mother) said she wanted to get a group of women together to learn to row, travel from New Zealand and compete in the Head of Yarra River race in Melbourne, Australia. Despite having rowed in a couple of parent races at summer camp with the boys and doing very, very badly in terms of rowing style, or even moving the boat forward, a number of us expressed interest. Fiona is an experienced rower and her enthusiasm filtered very quickly through to about fifteen of us. We joined up to begin to row as soon as possible.

So began my journey toward becoming a rower. I did the six session Learn to Row programme with the other Westlake mothers. The first session I was pretty nervous which seemed to be a common feeling for all the trainees. We used the learner boats. These are solid, stable boats that fit two people (we call them "fat doubles"). I thought that we would be going out in pairs but we got told we had to go out alone and do a circuit no further than the buoy. Golly, I thought. It's just going to be luck if I get out, around and back again. I have no idea how to steer a boat. My rowing partner offered to go first and I thought that was a jolly good idea. She did it well. Then it was my turn. "I can do this" I thought. And I did.

There was no skill involved during that first session. I can't say that it was good management that got me in and out of the pontoon and away from the bank. One of the ladies accidently pushed a swan out of the way when she drifted too close to the lake edge. She apologised to the swan as she was worried it would attack her. None of us ventured further than the buoys as our coach said she did not want to get a motor boat out to come and rescue us if we drifted toward the middle of the lake. That would definitely have been mortifying.

The Learn to Row programme was completed over three weekends. Very quickly we learnt terminology, positions, calls and so on. We were told to go to quarter slide, the catch, the finish. We got injuries, minor, but they were still rowing injuries. One day I came home with a big bruise on my back and had no idea what had caused it. I was concentrating on rowing and barely noticed anything else. I would get in the car after a row and have to think to turn the steering wheel and not pull harder on stroke side.

I remember asking one of the coaches early on "when can I call myself a rower?" "Now" she replied "because, you are". Wow! That was a pretty amazing moment. I am a rower, I am an athlete. I went home and told my husband "I'm a rower." I told my children and I told my friends. I even started to believe it a little bit myself. I have never been a sports person before. I had a horse and played tennis but that was not really serious sport. I envied my children for their rowing. The team camaraderie, the athleticism and now here it was my turn.

We graduated from the fat doubles to quads. It was terribly exciting to be in a real boat. Fiona was our coxswain and it was a great feeling to be able to row and not worry about what was around us. I could just concentrate on my stroke. Two of our crew were balancing the boat and the other two rowed, ideally together. That didn't always happen. We would get it and then someone would lose their way and we were back out of time again. However, being out there on the water was fantastic and Fiona was very gentle and positive with her comments. When we did get a stroke together it felt great.

The next step was to start feathering. I found that including that extra movement was just too much at times. Arms out, back straight, lean back, think about your position, think about your sequence, think about hands, elbows, head AND THEN feather the oar.

It worked, sometimes.

The Westlake barge was our next transition. This is two fours joined together by a platform where the coach and non-rowing squad members can sit. One of our coaches even put a couple of chairs there and sat comfortably drinking her coffee. We learnt how to row sweep oar on the barge. I enjoyed the sessions with all of us together. We didn't ever get the chance to take a picnic on-board but that would have been fun. Our time was spent working on technique and trying out pieces where the rowers would have a support person attempting to coach them. Remember we were all beginners!

About this time we were told that we should be doing ergs. My children had always groaned about the erg sessions. I was about to find out why. Our coach started us out with a few sessions where we didn't need to push ourselves too hard. One of our team even said she quite likes doing ergs. Then it stepped up. The coach laughed when we said the session was horrible. I came home and felt that my body was so exhausted I didn't have the energy to eat. I remember watching a programme about the Olympic rowers where they spoke about the amount of food they have to eat. They were saying they don't enjoy food a lot of the time. They eat just to fuel their body. Yes, that was me! Just having to fuel my body for the next session.

We went out in the four, quad, fat double or the barge. Then we graduated to an eight. The more experienced rowers from the club were starting to come out with us. Balance was our biggest issue and we went through a lot of exercises to attempt to keep the boat from tipping from side to side.

The first time we had all eight people rowing was thrilling for us all. That day we rowed twice around the lake. My daughter asked how rowing had gone when I got home. "How did your row go?" "Good" I said, "but I am a bit shattered". "Oh, how come, what did you do?" "We rowed twice around the lake". She looked at me and just laughed. The laugh of a rower who thinks twice around the lake is the beginning of a warm-up.

"Go and eat something" she said. "I don't feel hungry" I replied. "You need to eat to replenish your body. Even if you don't feel like it, you need to have something. Make a smoothie or something." Then she looked at me and shook her head "Creeps, this is so wrong. I feel like this is a role reversal. You are meant to be the mum!"

Another time I was rowing and putting a lot of energy into it. Unfortunately I caught a crab and was thrown to the edge of the boat and backwards straight into bow seat's arms. She laughed and gave me a hug. I wanted to just stay there feeling nurtured after I had been flung around the boat.

At times we have gone out on our own as a boat of novices. That can be pretty funny as we don't entirely know what we are doing. We have been told off for going the wrong way on the lake and for not being the right size for the boat we were rowing (I don't know that we could have done anything about that). We have had one person rowing into the pontoon while another is backing us away, one person in a boat giving the wrong instructions to another who seemed to get it anyway. Confusion with seat numbers and who is bow pair, what is bow side, and who is a bow side rower are frequent occurrences. One day I was rowing when the person behind me stopped to take off her jacket and then kept stopping to see where we needed to steer. The problem was that her oars kept slipping toward mine and I would come down with a stroke on top of her oar.

On land was also a place to make mistakes. We have carried the boat in the wrong way, put it in the shed back to front, left too few people holding the boat because we didn't understand where we were meant to stand and frequently take far too long sorting ourselves out.

Strangely, it is comforting to have the senior rowers telling us off. I feel as if I am back at school and there is someone in charge. When you have left school a long time ago this is rather nice as it is somewhere that I am learning while other people are more experienced. Being a mother and running a busy household means I always have to think and be responsible for other people.

Throughout our rowing journey we have felt much supported by our families. A number of our rowing children have coached the squad. My husband is ready to help with any maintenance when required and I always love to come home and share the morning's experiences with the rowers and ex-rowers at home. They guide and encourage me with questions and information and they listen to my stories. I am so lucky to move into the sport of rowing with a wonderful family and new friendships alongside me.

I'm sure Fiona wondered what on earth she had got herself into (probably still does). We are very grateful to her for starting this journey where we have new goals and challenges set that we are achieving week by week. Our biggest one yet is in two weeks. A large number of our Flying Swans squad have signed up to compete in our first regatta.

Jim Dietz

Jim is one of the great yarn-tellers in American Rowing. As an athlete he represented USA from 1969 to 1983 and then switched to coaching. He recently retired as head coach at the University of Massachusetts Womens Crew whose path is strewn with medals from 1996 to the present day.

That Will Cook Your Goose

One has to ask oneself, if you look at a sculling oar or a sweep oar blade, why are they the width that we see today? They could be made much thinner.

I can remember being over racing in the English Henley one year. There was an American four over there. I won't mention the guy in the boat because he's probably still traumatized, but they're coming down the Henley course, and there's a Canada goose swimming in the middle of the river.

All of a sudden, this guy makes contact with the goose's neck on the very thin blade edge and decapitates it. Well, that goose continued to swim around for the rest of the day, not realizing it lost its head.

Because of that, they went out and they made the rule that the blade had to be a little bit thicker.

Charlotte Pierce

Charlotte is a masters rower at Community Rowing Inc in Boston, Massachusetts USA and the host of the Ready, Row. USA! Podcast. Jim Dietz is a former US athlete and coach. He is the author of the tale "That Will Cook Your Goose" elsewhere in this book.

Jim Dietz And The Alligator

It's the dead of winter in Boston, and after six weeks of indoor erg classes, I decide what I need is a week in Florida. So I sign up for the mid-January All American Rowing Camp session in DeLand.

After a few days of coaching input, "Slow up the slide, Charlotte!," a few of my fellow campers and I head out with Jim Dietz, across Lake Beresford and up the cypress-lined banks of the Dead River. The other contingent heads out with Mark Wilson, up the St John River.

Jim's in a mellow mood, not inclined to do a whole lot of direct coaching or critique today. He points out the occasional subtropical bird, small alligator, clutch of turkeys, and manatee ripple along the course, along with a side of philosophy and Olympic rowing stories. Under the warm Florida sun, we're in a Dietz-induced zen rowing steady-state.

After turning around and aiming back along the river toward second breakfast, I spot a large alligator sunning itself along the bank, then a small alligator nearby which I imagined to be her baby. Despite her size, she was well camouflaged under her chosen cypress. Ever handy with his handheld coaching device, aka smartphone, Jim takes this picture of me in front of the alligator.

Whereupon I decide to fish out my own smartphone for some closer photos. Who knows, I could get them on Instagram before I get back to the dock!

As I paw through my pack, my boat drifts closer to the water lilies along the shore, disturbing them ever so slightly. Suddenly, the mighty alligator lifts her massive head and makes a mad dash, straight toward me into the river!

Who knows if that gigantic creature is actually coming for me, but I am not sticking around to find out. That's when I activate all my previous coaching and distill it into one focused effort to get down the river as fast and efficiently as I can. About 500 meters later, I stop and Jim and the others catch up.

"Charlotte, that has to be the fastest racing start I've ever seen you do," was Jim's assessment. "Just wish I had it on video, but I couldn't get my phone back out fast enough!"

Who cares how fast I rushed the slide?

Tidying The Tideway

Reddit has an active rowing group, and people comment there under pseudonyms. I picked up this rowing tale from a delightful discussion authored by the contributor called "Tidying The Tideway".

The Magic Of Three Seat?

My team jiggled the crew order a bit last week for a session, and I ended up in three seat. (That's what I tell myself, but the likely reality is that I just couldn't sit anywhere else.)

A friend of mine once told me that if the rest of the crew is good enough, it doesn't actually matter what three man does in the boat. I decided to test this theory out for myself.

The first opportunity came in the warm up, when we were rowing in fours. Once convinced that the boat was moving in a somewhat constant speed through the drive, I lowered my applied watts down by approximately 35.7% - the boat was still moving at the same speed as before. I loosened my legs further, dropping the power down by a further 45.8%. Still the same speed. Although I was shocked, I instinctively thought that the rest of the crew who were rowing were increasing their power as I was decreasing mine, and I told myself that that was the case.

When we moved on to full-on work pieces, I thought - if the boat speed doesn't change if I lower the power through my drive, how about if I catch a crab? And that is what I did. I checked that my footplate was secure, and that my feet were firmly in my shoes, because one thing I did not want was an ejector crab into the muddy Tideway water. Guess what? The boat speed was still the same. In fact, I'm pretty sure we were moving faster than when I was rowing "properly".

Before I concluded that my friend's statement was true, there was one more test that I needed to carry out. After the pieces, we moved on to some technical exercises, mainly pausing ones. Half slide, blades off the water, I let go of my handle whilst everyone else was setting the boat. I took my feet out of my shoes, and made the grave mistake of sitting in the footwell. As I jumped up, my legs fell through the hull, but I was determined to finish what I had started, and I threw myself up and did a mid-air somersault. I landed perfectly, and quickly put my feet back in, oar in hands.

This was when I gasped.

As I returned to my original half slide position, I realised that the boat was perfectly set. Not only that, but the hole I made in the boat had disappeared.

I am now fully convinced that nothing you do in three seat makes any effect to the boat. Has anyone else had this experience?

Noel Donaldson

Noel has coached two of the most successful pairs athletes of recent times - both Olympic medalists and multiple world-medalists. In this tale he reflects on the similarities between an Australian and a New Zealander.

Bowmen Can Multi-Task

Drew Ginn and Eric Murray are completely different human beings, but both have sat in the bow seat of a very successful pair.

Drew won it with James Tompkins. He did it with Duncan Free too.

Eric did it with Hamish Bond.

In last year's *Rowing Tales (2018)* there was a story about how Drew Ginn could call the race and he could also multitask through the middle of the Atlanta Olympic Games final. That's where the similarity with Eric Murray actually was. You know, Drew had a wonderful ability through talent; Eric through his inherent abilities to multitask.

I always said that Eric Murray in a pair could steer the boat as straight as anybody in the world. He could light a cigarette up halfway, take a phone call, and not miss a beat. He just had this ability to multitask in the boat better than anybody.

Doing team workouts, he could cut a swathe through the group. He could look over his shoulder and he would know that we're in a wake. How do I get out of the wake? I go over there. It is a wonderful ability to be able to multitask!

Having a bowman like that in a race to be able to call the shots, particularly when you've got your nose in front, to be able to look and see where you were, and to be able to give his partner lots of reassurance, he had that wonderful ability, and Drew had that same ability at the same time as well.

Drew and James Tompkins were very advanced in their mental skill ability. We did a bit of visualization and the like in our training. Working with our sports psychologist, we thought, "We're just getting a bit boring doing the same old, same old."

We were always looking for different ways to come at it. Usually, when you do a visualization session or a progressive muscle relaxation session, athletes are in that relaxed trance and they lie there and a coach or coxswain in a big boat might call a race.

But Drew had that ability to be super relaxed but aware, and I could talk them through starting a race. He could then call the race. I could then lead him through where the opposition were and he would call the race and suchlike there, too.

In a super relaxed trance-type of state there, he still had the ability to be able to be aware and to call and yet be really relaxed. You could draw him back into a relaxed state again.

And so, the two bowmen of the undefeated Olympic pairs for the last four or five Olympic Games both had such great similar attributes of being able to be super aware of their surroundings and the like.

There are some differences between the two people. But, in the end, there is the same end result of bowmen being able to command races.

Caroline Buckley

The London Daily Telegraph newspaper had a gossip column called "Peterborough" until 2003. It was authored for many years by Robert Hardman, now a distinguished newspaperman, when he was a rookie. Robert was a university friend of Caroline Buckley - who rowed twice for Cambridge in the Women's Boat Race in 1986 and 1987. The National Championships were after university term ended and so keeping a crew together and training for a month after exams was a challenge. They had to take every opportunity they could to train.

Rowing On Hallowed Waters

It's now 1987. We have decided we're going to compete in the UK National Championships. The whole world has gone to race at Henley Royal Regatta, but women are not allowed to row at Henley.

We were watching the regatta and went to the boat tent and pleaded with the boys from our club. "Can we borrow your boat, please? Because we'd like to go out and practice for the nationals."

It was basically dusk, twilight, so we thought we'd just go row the course for practice, and we did.

We got the boat out. They lent it to us. We went down and rowed the course, we got it timed, and we beat most of the boats who had rowed that day.

I think we went to a party that evening. We partied hard.

Robert Hardman came up to me at the party and says, "Caroline, what have you been doing today?" I said, "Well, we just rowed the Henley course, and we rowed it faster than many of those boats at the Regatta today."

The next day in the Peterborough Column appears. "Caroline Buckley says women are better than men. They rowed the course, the hallowed course, under cover of darkness..."

Alan Campbell

Alan Campbell rowed for Great Britain from 2003 to 2016. An exuberant Northern Irishman, Alan enjoyed the underdog position as a little-known competitor until after the Henley win he describes here. He was encouraged in this by his coach, Bill Barry. Bill was an Olympic Silver Medalist in 1964 and together with Alan reignited his country's competitiveness in heavy mens single sculling. Olaf Tufte represented Norway in single and double sculls winning 4 Olympic medals from 2000 - 2016. He is still competing in FISA regattas in 2019.

The Race For The Ages

The two best races I ever had at Henley were not finals; they were both semi-finals.

In the Diamond Sculls semi-finals of 2003, I was up against Simon Goodbrand. He was from Cambridge and at the end of his rowing career. This was his last opportunity to try and win the Diamonds.

I'd come in from the qualifiers – I am still the first person to ever come through Henley qualifiers to win that trophy. I had dyed my hair yellow and red that year to match my club colours and so I was very noticeable on the water.

In the race he was leading me right up towards the very end. Bill [Barry] and I had worked on my sprint – and I did the big old sprint.

And so I did come through him to win.

There's a brilliant picture of Simon watching me overtake him just in the last bits of the race as well. I like that photo.

At that point, that was a big transformational shift in my thinking in terms of the single scull. Knowing it was where I wanted to be. When I got my opportunity in 2006 to be the British single sculler, that was all part and parcel of me then going on to win the first World Cup in Munich.

My second favourite race, again, was the Diamond Sculls semi-finals against Olaf Tufte in 2009. Obviously, there were quite a few internationals that had come to race that year, post-Olympics. So Mahe Drysdale (New Zealand) was on the other side of the draw against Tim Maeyens (Belgium).

It was Olaf's first time out at Henley Royal Regatta. Again, it was one of those races where we exchanged leads. First I led, then he led, I led, he led, and then it looked like he was getting the better of me.

Just as we came alongside the competitor's enclosure, the crowd just really lifted me. I took the rate up and managed to get through him, and this was one of those big epic races.

In the umpire's boat behind me, I had Bill, my Dad was there, and my first ever coach, Sid Grey who had coached me down at my school boat club in Coleraine, Northern Ireland.

Afterwards Sid came out, beamed his smile, and said it was the best race he'd ever seen me do, the best race he'd ever seen at Henley. It was one of those things that people came up to me afterwards and said, "That was a race for the ages".

Bryan Kitch

As many people know the rules of gentleman's dress in the UK is complex. There are a lot of rules that a non-Briton can break unwittingly. And for one American coming to compete at Henley Royal Regatta for the first time, going into the Stewards' Enclosure after racing was almost as nerve-wracking as the actual race.

Bryan Kitch is the author of the Rowing Related monthly newsletter and blog, he contributes to Row2k and Row360 magazine and is now a very experienced Henley Royal competitor.

Sometimes, Always, Never

The first time I went to Henley, I went with the New York Athletic Club in a Wyfold Challenge Cup four and one of the folks that was in that crew was Rob Milam who is now fairly high up in US Rowing.

He had rowed for Princeton and competed for the New York AC for a lot of years. It was not his first trip but it was mine. And he always kind of went out of his way to take me under his wing a little bit.

I actually didn't bring with me any of the appropriate clothes to go into the Stewards 'Enclosure.

Fortunately, as we were a lightweight crew, we were all basically the same size. Rob gave me effectively a full attire, suit jacket, pants, shirt, including shoes. I showed up the first day in Stewards and I had buttoned my jacket up. He just looks at me and shakes his head.

Rob points at the three buttons on my coat jacket and he moves his finger down the buttons, "Sometimes, always, never."

I just look at that as one of those moments when I had to laugh at myself. Also, again, an example of him kind of showing me the ropes in as nice a way as he could.

Chris Madell

Chris Madell started coxing at Oxford in 1974, did Blues trials in 1977-78 and wound up coxing the University lightweight VIII. He tells me "I actually gave it up before the race against Cambridge as there was so much in-fighting in the crew it was no longer fun."

Andrew Probert is a former Cambridge University coxswain who still graces the stern of many masters crews. He is an expert at steering the River Thames in London, called the Tideway because it's tidal. Chris Madell is Andrew's friend and fellow coxswain - he tells this tale.

Choose Your Friends Carefully

Mercifully I still have a pair of wellies. I thought I'd given up coxing for good, and so when a dear friend of mine started rowing in Amsterdam a couple of years back, I'd sent her my rather spiffy Tideway Scullers School splash top, and a rather hideous, if effective, pair of TSS tracksuit bottoms. Fortunately when I gave up coxing lycra was only just coming in, as I would not look good in it.

I got a rather oblique message from Andrew Probert a while back saying "I may have volunteered you for some coxing duty". This was a Saturday evening.

I didn't think anything of it until I get a call on the Sunday from someone called Steve at Quintin Boat Club. He explained that Andrew had agreed to cox a Quintin Masters' VIII in the Quintin Head the following Saturday and realised that he had to be at a wedding in Brighton that day. He had thrown my name in the frame, and would I consider doing it?

I asked Steve to let me think about it overnight. And replied saying if they were really stuck I'd do it. But pointed out that I hadn't actually coxed that stretch in over twenty-five years, and I am not as light as I once was. But I'd be more than happy to help them find someone better suited to the task.

I pulled every string I could think of to find a substitute. But no luck. Long story short, I wound up coxing them and we did okay winning Masters F by some 12 seconds.

Fast forward to early February. Out of the blue I get an email from Mostyn Lewis from Ardingly Rowing Club. Would I be interested in coxing the Ardingly women's crew in the Women's Head, with the possibility of doing a practice race at the Hammersmith Head? Apparently Andrew had yet again recommended me for rather complicated reasons.

I replied with the usual caveats, that they may well be able to find someone lighter and with more recent Tideway experience than myself. Apparently they couldn't. So, feeling sick as a dog, I drag my ass out of bed at 6.30 on a Sunday morning to make my way over to Putney.

I wind up sitting in this borrowed Vespoli eight which was not designed for me, nor I for it. I'm not that tall, being about 5' 9" but I swear it was the most uncomfortable boat I have ever sat in. Given the amount of clothing I had on, I could barely find the steering toggles nor see the cox box screen. After about fifteen minutes given my height and width constraints, both my legs were numb. It was the first time I have ever had to be lifted out of a boat at the end of an outing because I couldn't stand. I've been lifted out and thrown in the water before, but this was somewhat different.

I called the Ardingly coach a couple of days later saying that unless they could find a different boat, I certainly could not cox the Women's Head.

As luck would have it, they managed to find a gal; I'm glad they did.

As Andrew later sagely pointed out, Louise (whose last name happens to be Cox) will be lighter, sharper and better looking than either of us...

I do miss the sport, particularly the camaraderie.

Gloria DiFulvio

Gloria DiFulvio splits her life between being a rower in the early morning, a public health academic by day, and a storyteller by night. She is a writer of creative nonfiction and has published stories in *Huffington Post*, *Ravishly* and *The Sunlight Press* (forthcoming) and lives with her wife, Australian Shepherd, and cat in rural Hadley Massachusetts, USA. She is a masters rower with Northampton Community Rowing, Northampton, MA, USA.

I'm OK With Mediocrity

I've never been an athlete. At 5'4" and a weight I won't reveal, (though I can safely say that I'm off the standardized charts for BMI). I have always considered myself absolutely average in most realms athletic. I'm content to be the last in a pack of road cyclists. I'm used to being way behind my peers as I traverse trails on my mountain bike. I'm happy to finish a 5k in the middle of the pack as long as I'm upright. At least I think I am OK with mediocrity.

The secret is that I'm also fiercely competitive. I try to keep this part of me hidden, but people who know me well see that while I feign contentment with my middle-of-the road self, I desperately wish otherwise.

I took up a new adventure almost six years ago at the age of 46: rowing.

 While I consider myself adept at most things, this has been the most physically and emotionally challenging endeavor yet. Three mornings a week for seven months a year, at the wee small hour of 5:30 am, I get into a boat with either three or seven other men and women to propel a small thin craft down a river.

Confronting my inadequacies on the water has put me face to face with the same fears and inadequacies I face in life. How do I sit with my mistakes that so obviously not only affect me, but the whole boat? How do I make small changes that, while barely noticeable, have a profound effect on the success of the row?

When I signed up to learn this sport and immerse myself in its lessons I had no idea that I was giving myself a gift that would serve me well as I took the inevitable steps towards 50.

Several years ago, friends and I made a crazy decision to drive nine hours from Massachusetts to Cleveland Ohio for three days duration and a total of 12 minutes of athletic competition. We entered the Gay Games rowing competition.

Each race takes about 5–6 minutes to complete, but those minutes feel like the hardest minutes of my life. Still new to rowing, I had tremendous fear about my ability to compete. I had spent little time in the smaller coxed four, a boat considerably less stable than the larger eight that I was used to rowing. Did I mention I have a healthy, but exaggerated, fear of water?

The Cuyahoga River in Cleveland is a curvy, narrow river with large shipping boats meandering down it quite often. Once you launch your shell, if a large vessel is coming, you must give way, which means sitting for well, a long time. Water reverberates against high river walls making even the most seaworthy a little nauseous. My teammates and I began our row to the starting line. Shortly after we launch, this is where we find ourselves, sitting idly by in the hot sun waiting for multiple large, slow boats to clear the course. My anxiety intensifies.

Eventually making it to the start line, we are given the clearance to start. "Ready all, Row!" is the familiar starting call for a race. And we're off. While the Gay Games is an open competition, meaning you don't have to qualify to participate, it was a big deal to me! My non-athletic, content-to-be-last, outer self has traversed halfway across the country to compete in this international competition. But the fierce competitor inside me takes over. I want nothing more than to win.

With less-than a stellar start, our boat is far behind. Our coxswain, bold and brave, makes the right calls to keep our head and heart in the race even though we have seemingly already lost. About halfway into the 1,500 meter race, we approach a turn, and our coxswain yells, "They're only a boat length ahead of us!"

We cannot give up.

And that's when I find my real inner competitor. Each of us reach deep down inside for those last 750 meters. At 1,000 meters our boat is now overlapping the other boat. Our muscles cry, our hearts pound as we've decided, each of us independently, that we're not going home without a medal. As we turn the corner, we hear the crowd yell and make our move. Dead even with our competitor. As we cross that finish line, in the closest event of the competition, the deafening cheers tell me: I am an athlete.

Here, I've accomplished something greater than a gold medal. I didn't give up. Despite my fear, my disbelief in myself, and a race start that seemed to predict the ending before it arrived, I fought. I fought for myself and my teammates.

And we won.

Michael d'Eredita

Michael is a Professor at Syracuse University, New York, USA teaching entrepreneurship, innovation and creativity. He is also the High Performance Director for the Portuguese Rowing Federation. His professional life has flexed between academia and rowing and his enthusiasm for both allows ideas, concepts and expertise to flow between the two.

A Heart-Felt Rowing Life

I have a rowing tale, but it's less of a specific story, and a little bit more of a storyline that's continuing to play out, and it's related to Portugal. It has to do with a relationship.

I would say it's less of a rowing story to watch and more of a story of an individual who is full of heart – a heart that I first saw on the water and a heart that started to be translated into the heart of an entrepreneur.

Luis Teixeira is the president of the Portuguese Rowing Federation. I coached Luis in 2003 and 2004 and we've become great friends since.

After 2004, he went on and he started a training centre – Avizaqcua in Portugal. It's become quite the place and has attracted a large number of high-performance teams which was always his vision for this place.

When I went to coach the Portuguese national rowing team in 2003, I spent a lot of time up in the north of Portugal. A lot of the athletes were from Porto – except for Luis who is from Lisbon, south of Avizaqcua.

He kept saying, "You need to come down. You need to come down and check out this place called Avis – the countryside of Portugal." And so eventually I said, "Okay, let's do it. Let's go down to Avis."

On the train to Avis, there was one place we stopped at for a little while before we got there. I said, "This place is like a dream". Literally, you had to pinch yourself even when you're in it. Beyond the flat water, the scenery, all of it was just strangely idyllic.

He said, "You haven't seen Avis."

And so, we ended up going over to Avis for a training camp. That's when I remember walking down to the lake shore with him and just looking at it and him explaining to me how the water was, the direction of the water, the amount of water, and all of it, then me looking at him, saying, "People would come from all over the world to row at this place".

He'd been cooking up an idea to build this training centre already. What was there before? Nothing. Farmland. There was nothing there except his vision.

Luis built the team up, he got the resources. He did all the entrepreneurial things you need to do in order to literally create something out of nothing.

Now, the real story of this place, I think, and the most interesting part is less about the rowing training and more about when you go to dinner or when you're in the off times at camp and you're drinking wine around the table and you've got people from all over the world – from all of these different rowing cultures and all these different places – and you're just talking rowing or politics or whatever.

It has this community that's there of people sharing.

It's fantastic. It's hard to describe Avis as just a place because there's so much community dynamic and behaviour that's layered with all these multicultural perspectives and rowing know-how and all these other things that come into it.

And the storyline is still playing out.

You know, I hope others tune into it because it's a fascinating one in terms of what he's built – even beyond the centre but also what he's built in terms of his life. Luis is an individual who now interacts with the highest-performing rowing teams in the world on a regular basis. He even rows and trains with them when he wants to.

He's built a life around this passion for rowing that is admirable on many levels, so that would be my storyline – the continuing storyline that I would like to put forth as my rowing tale.

Martin Cross

Martin is a rowing author, journalist and World Rowing race commentator. You hear his voice on the World Cup and World Championships broadcast each year. He says he is the longest-serving member of the British Rowing Team ever.

We're All At Sea Here

I was rowing a coxed four. It was John Maxey, Adam Clift, myself and John Garrett. We were trying out for the Seoul Olympics in 1988.

We used to go to Sabaudia, in Italy for training camp. Sabaudia is a lake well-known by a lot of nations and the Italian team train there and they stay on the beach by the sea.

We went there, the trailer rocked up, and the hotel is on the beachfront, so the Mediterranean is just out on one side of the road and the rowing course on the other side. People had to get their boats off the trailer and take them over to the rowing lake and basically go out rowing. It was the first outing of camp.

It happened, that John and I were a bit late to come down from breakfast, and we were the last pair to take our boat off the trailer. As we got there we were kind of looking out to the sea; the sea was like an absolute millpond. There were no waves whatsoever.

We just looked at each other and we just thought, you know, because I'm a bit of a rebel, and John Garrett was up for it, and we just thought, "Should we go rowing on the sea?"

So, basically, we rigged up the boat and we left our shoes on the beach – like a kind of warning because we didn't tell anyone which was probably a bit stupid.

We just went out, and you could see a boat in the far distance, but these things always look closer. And so we rowed towards that boat. We probably went out about 10 kilometres into the Mediterranean Sea. You could see the big mountain at Sabaudia, you could see that was getting quite small.

We rowed and then we kind of just stopped. We didn't quite get to the boat because I think we started to bottle it. There was no wind. But, when we stopped, I looked at my rigger and the top nut had come completely out and it was just about to fall in the sea.

I thought, "Shit! We were just out in the middle of the sea!"

Luckily, we got back safely, but it was both one of the most amazing experiences and one of the most silly things to do because we were part of the Olympic team. It was one of the most memorable things – the only time I've ever been coastal rowing on the Mediterranean.

I treasure that memory and that time rowing on the Mediterranean.

Aly Mielbrandt and Tonia Williams

Tonia Williams rowed for Great Britain in women's lightweight coxless fours, and was in the first ever British women's sweep crew to win a World Gold medal. Aly Mielbrandt (neé Overy) raced for the United States in 1992 and 1993. They now both live in Auckland, New Zealand. This tale is about the 1993 World Championships in Račice, Czech Republic. The medal ceremony at the World Rowing Championships has each crew walk up in crew order - from stroke to bow with the gold medalists in the centre of the podium, silver and bronze on either side.

We Last Met On The Podium

TONIA: Our rowing tale is about decades' old reunions.

We were both unbeknown to each other going to North Shore Rowing Club's Prize giving in 2013.

People on our table told me, "Oh, there's a former USA international rower who's going to be coming to prize giving. You'll know her – Aly."

The name didn't sound familiar to me - it went straight over the top of my head.

Anyway, I sat at the top table because I was Club President at the time, and I stood up, shook hands and introduced myself and said, "Hi. I'm Tonia." And Aly said, "I know!"

She sat next to me and I sat down thinking, "How does she know? Who is she? Is she a spy? I don't know any Americans."

ALY: I think we must have been talking about rowing pedigree. Yes, I must have been thinking "Oh, I want to sit next to this wonderful woman who is an amazing rower because she crushed me in 1993."

TONIA: The back story is that the last time we had been next to each other – was on the podium at the World Rowing Championships in '93. We were literally right next to each other because you were bow with the US four.

ALY: Yes, and we got the bronze medal. And you were stroke of the GB crew that got the gold medal.

TONIA: Apart from maybe swapping some uniform in the boat park after racing, we literally hadn't seen each other for 20 years. And then – blow me – of all the places, you end up at my little club on my little lake.

ALY: I have the picture of that medal ceremony on my desk. I think I cut you out.

Bill Mitchell

The 1986 World Rowing Championships were held in Nottingham, UK and it was all hands to the pump to ensure a successful event was held. FISA likes to provide commentary in several languages and in those days multi-lane umpires all used French to start the racing.

Stan Collingwood was a distinguished coach and umpire from Thames Tradesmens Rowing Club in London, UK. His skill at improving the way regattas were umpired and marshalled with crews "stacked above the start" revolutionised racing for the Fours Head of the River and was adopted by most other London head races. This story is told by his good friend and club-mate, Bill Mitchell.

We're Abreast

During the 1986 World Championships, the person who was doing the French element of commentating did not turn up. Typical Stan, a good boy scout, said he would do it. Stan does not speak French.

He got someone to write the script for him to read out over the loudspeaker system.

During the women's quad race the crews were very tight at the front of the field. Stan gave this strangled schoolboy French description of a very close race.

After the race had finished, some of the French spectators came to the commentary box asking "Why did he say that the two leading crews are massaging their breasts?"

Anonymous

London's River Thames is one of the most famous rowing rivers of the world. The place where the annual Oxford and Cambridge Boat Race is fought, the place where the split between professional watermen and amateur oarsmen used to maintain a separation between people who shared a love for rowing. Today it is home to many rowing clubs, particularly on the tidal portion of the river below the Richmond half lock - this holds back the outgoing tide so that the good burghers of the Royal Borough of Richmond Upon Thames do not have to look out onto mud banks at low tide.

The Tideway is the colloquial expression used to describe the fully tidal portion of the river. I am told that the tidal ranges experienced around the British Isles are among the largest in the world - 6 meters and more happen every lunar cycle in the Port of London. Add in the flow of a large river and the speed of water moving downstream is high.

When Tea And Toast Kept The Coni Rules

I want to tell you a story about how a club transformed itself.

The club I'm talking about is one in London, probably well-known to a lot of people. It used to be the place where arrogance ruled, and who-shouts-loudest won all the arguments.

It contained a range of different training groups – school children of different ages, adult men, women, recreational rowers and masters. Each had their own priorities and areas of focus and used to squabble regularly over who got the newest equipment, who got the "best" coaches, and who got the preferred training times in the gym and access to the water.

But that all changed, and the club made a remarkable transformation towards becoming a place of consideration and respect for each training group's members. In this story, I want to tell you about how we made that shift, and the unexpected prize that we won as a result.

It all began when the London Tideway Harbour Master announced a water safety review. The gentleman in question had apparently been standing on Hammersmith Bridge in West London, looking at the River Thames, on a busy Saturday in March. He was watching the ebb and flow of rowing boats practicing for the forthcoming Head of the River Race.

The river in London, because it's tidal, flows out for around eight hours for every four hours that it flows in. A rowing boat, particularly one manned by someone who is not very strong, cannot row in the middle of the river against the tide because the tide flows too quickly.

Just for background, the tidal range on the Tideway is between 3.5 and five metres each day. That's one of the highest in the world. And so, you can imagine at peak flow, when there's also river water heading out towards the sea, it moves very quickly indeed.

As a result, the tidal Thames has navigation rules which are unique. In every other river, water craft pass "port to port". That means people row like traffic on a road – up one lane in one direction, and down the other side of the river in the other direction.

On the tidal Thames, this is different because when they want to row upriver against the stream, they do this in the shallows where the stream is weakest. This is known as "working the slacks".

And so, an experienced rower and barrister, Peter Coni, documented what are now known as the Coni Rules. These determine the places in the river where it is safe to row in the shallows going upstream when the tide is flowing out; the places where there are obstacles such as piers and moored boats which prevent that progress and necessitate the crew to cross the river and row up the opposite foreshore.

When the tide turns, these rules reverse.

What the Harbour Master saw from the bridge at Hammersmith horrified him. He happened to be watching the practice sessions on the river one week before the largest eights race in the UK. It's called the Head of the River. In it, over 350 crews race the University Course – from Mortlake to Putney – one after the other in a timed piece.

Because it was the week before, everybody was doing intense high-speed, high-rating practices. Inevitably, some boats were faster than others. And so, there were big strong men in fast-moving boats overtaking each other in the middle of the river, cutting corners and forcing other craft to the side of the river in order to avoid collision.

Under Hammersmith Bridge, the Thames is reasonably wide. It's wide enough that three boats can row side by side and all of them get the benefit of the stream. The Harbour Master was shocked because he believed that this was extremely dangerous behaviour.

As a result, he worked to force a water safety review by The Salvage Association which sought to reintroduce the traditional port-to-port navigation rules and which would have effectively caused the death knell of rowing on the tidal Thames.

The rowing response to this review was coordinated by Stan Collingwood (about whom Bill Mitchell's Rowing Tale, "We're Abreast", is published elsewhere in this book).

On 23 October 2004 he wrote to the clubs "The Tideway is a precious legacy which I would like to pass for future generations to enjoy. Please help me in this quest".

Once the review was underway, my club was visited by a representative of the review panel who, after our training on a Sunday lunchtime, rolled out a large sheet of paper onto the table in our club room.

Chris and I, as representatives of the club, sat and listened to their proposals. We tried in vain to explain to them that a 10-year-old in a single scull – which is, by definition, a not particularly strong athlete rowing in the slowest rowing boat – would be unable at peak tide to pass around a pier or a moored boat because the force of the flow of water in the opposite direction would move them backwards, not forwards.

During our discussion, my colleague Chris looked very closely at the map that was in front of us. It had all the bridges marked, it had a lot of the shallows of the river marked, and some of the landmarks. He turned to me and remarked, "This must be a jolly old map because they haven't got the new Kew Records Office on it." With disdain, the Harbour Master's representative replied, "This isn't a map. It's a nautical chart." Chris and I were suitably put in our place.

The water safety review, as I recall, involved a period when the Harbour Master allowed rowing clubs to continue to row following the Coni Rules but all accidents, incidents, and near misses had to be recorded. It would be determined after this period whether or not the rowers were to be allowed to continue rowing on the Tideway.

The Harbour Master added some buoys to the river in order to force boats closer to the shoreline at places where they perceived congestion was likely to occur – for example, near Hammersmith Bridge. It was also announced that there would be a prize given to the club who behaved the best and had the fewest incidents.

How did my club change to becoming a considerate place where each training group enjoyed its relationship with the other training groups?

Firstly, obviously, we all were told very strictly that we had to adhere to the safety rules or else the club would be fined, and potentially the sport could be banned. Obviously, that brought a new sense of realism to how people chose to behave during their training.

The second thing – and the more remarkable part of it – was a simultaneous and unrelated decision to offer tea and coffee to everybody at weekends between their outings. Now, the club had a very, very small kitchen. In the past, we had operated an honesty box system whereby each athlete went into the kitchen, boiled the kettle, and made themselves a cup of tea or coffee. If they had brought their own bread, they could make toast.

This changed when we opened in the bar in the main club room and organised a rota whereby each training group took it in turn to staff the bar and to serve the tea, coffee, and toast.

This sounds trivial, but what was interesting was the outcome. Previously, once we had made a drink, we tended to sit around a table, talking to our contemporaries in our training group. And so, there were isolated groups of athletes, each holding their own conversations.

After the catering was moved into the bar area and every training group was forced to come face-to-face with every other member of the club – at least once every two months – and say to them, "Hello! Would you like tea or coffee?" and take their order. People began to recognize each other, they began to say hello to each other, and they began to have conversations that were a little more extensive than their food order.

As a result, we began to get to know other people. Once we got to know people, we started to respect them and to understand their training priorities and to become more flexible in our approach to each other's needs and wants.

While the water safety review continued, the club was exemplary in its behaviour. When the results of the review were announced by the water safety advisor, all the other clubs declared that it must have been a fluke because my club was the one given a prize for being the safest club on the Tideway. We laughed, but underneath we knew the reason this had happened was because we all now drank our tea and ate our toast together.

Judy Rantz Williams

Judy is the daughter of Joe Rantz. He won Olympic gold in 1936 at the Berlin Olympics in the US Eight and is the central character of Dan Brown's bestselling book, The Boys in the Boat.

I was introduced to Judy by her daughter, Jennifer Huffman who took up rowing later in life and much to her own sadness, long after her grandfather had died. She wishes she could have talked rowing tales with him.

A Daughter Remembers – The Story Behind The *Boys In The Boat*

I have often wished for a time machine. A DeLorean I think. I wanted a way to go back into the past and observe what things were like before my time or to relive those times I loved. One thing I had always yearned for was to see my parents grow up. I had heard stories of course — snippets in time. I knew their journey had been harsh, but I also knew it had been amazing. At some level I think I have always felt this longing, this need, to watch my Dad as he first learned how to survive — and then learned how to live.

I wanted to see him at that amazing Moment when the 1936 Washington Varsity crew finally comes together and the boat explodes with power. To watch them race, not just glean what I could from some flickering black and white newsreels, but to see it, in full color, to hear it. I guess what I really wanted was to fully understand the experience and live it with Dad. I had always wanted that, but of course it wasn't possible — until I met Daniel James Brown.

In 2004, when my Dad turned 90, he finally had to sell his house. While my daughter and sister were cleaning out the attic they came across a trove of rowing memorabilia. There were scrapbooks, newspaper articles, postcards, rowing shirts, train schedules — an amazing assortment of stuff from my Dad's university years. My daughter, Jennifer, immediately realized the historical importance of these materials and she took on the task of archiving everything into a chronological and narrated scrapbook.

I had always known there was a story to be told about my Dad and the crew, but I guess I always figured it was "big" enough and "important" enough that one of the many people who came buzzing around over the years and interviewing Dad and the guys would eventually write something and that would take care of it. But the years passed and nothing happened. Those men who had made the history were dying off and I could feel the threads of the story slipping away. And then I saw what Jennifer had put together, and the vision of how to approach writing the story became much more clear. I began to wonder whether I was the person to preserve the Legend.

And so I set out on a mission with Dad to collect whatever odds and ends of memories he happened to spontaneously think about. I followed him around with a pad and pencil for over three years. So when a request came to Dad from a history teacher in Indiana, I wrote up a nine-page synopsis of Dad's life and the crew's history that looked pretty good. I was beginning to think I might write the story.

In the meantime, Daniel James Brown moved into our neighborhood. I had met him a number of times at our homeowners 'association meetings. He was in the process of writing his first book. When it was published in 2006, he encouraged us to buy it and read it, with the promise that he would sign it. Well, I bought it. I read it. Under a Flaming Sky. And it transported me back to Hinckley, Minnesota into a raging firestorm in 1894. I could see the town. I could hear the roar of the approaching fire. I could practically feel the flames licking at the windows of the train as it attempted to outrun the inferno. And it hit me. I didn't need a time machine! The answer was staring me right in the face!

OK, so there were a few questions to be answered. Would Dad feel like I did about the way Dan writes a story? Would he even agree to have his story written? Would Dan want to write it? Could he transport me into Dad's past the way he transported me into that firestorm in Hinckley? And the answer to all those questions, eventually, was "Yes".

I will have to admit a couple of things. First, that when I started this whole mission my motives were basically selfish. I didn't want Dad's memory forgotten. I didn't want forgotten what those boys accomplished. And, I suppose, I also hoped that the examples of what they had to go through, might make some people consider whether their own situation was really all that tough.

Second, I had no inkling of the journey Dan and I would be embarking on. I'm not even sure he realized completely where we were headed. It was pretty much a six-year odyssey of research and writing. Of outreach, questions and discoveries – because in order to make the story live, the boys had to be in a background the reader understood. In order to get the full gut wrenching impact of it, you had to be there – with Joe and the Boys. You had to feel as though you were seeing what they saw...taking the journey with them. And that is Dan's gift to me – to all of us.

In our current world, where national teams are made up of oarsmen and women throughout the country, and where college teams are regularly made up of people recruited throughout the world, it is an almost inconceivable thought that the nine boys in the Husky Clipper all came from western Washington — and that none had set foot in a racing shell before they arrived on campus.[1]

So let's take a look at who these Boys were and where they came from. I'll begin with the four that came from Seattle.

At bow was Roger Morris. Roger grew up in the Fremont district about two and half miles west of the University. Like many others,

---

[1] The Husky Clipper is the name of the boat they raced in at the Olympic Games.

his family had been solid middle class until the Great Depression. They still held onto their family-owned moving business, but life was now a struggle. Roger earned his tuition money playing in a dance band.

In seat #2 was Chuck Day. He was probably the most financially stable of the group. His home was just a few blocks north of the University campus. His father was a dentist, and as my Dad observed Chuck was the best dressed guy of the lot. So why did he turn out for crew? Maybe to follow in the footsteps of his older brother, Herb, who had rowed Varsity a few years earlier. But I suspect it was just because he loved a challenge. Anyone who would voluntarily choose to work a summer on a job as tough and dangerous as the Grand Coulee Dam had to have the tenacity of a bulldog.[2]

In seat #4 was Johnny White. He grew up in south Seattle along Lake Washington. His family was one of the many who had lost most everything in the Depression. When he graduated from high school two years early, where his only extracurricular activity had been playing violin in the school orchestra, he was neither fully grown nor fully filled out. If he was to fulfil his father's dream for him and become an oarsman, he needed to put on years and muscle — and also somehow earn the money for tuition before he approached the University. And so, after two years of heavy labor on the docks and at a lumber yard, he arrived at the University of Washington tall, fully muscled, and with tuition money to keep him in school — at least for a while.

In seat #5 was Jim "Stub" McMillin. Stub grew up in Seattle on Queen Anne Hill. From early on his life outside school was taken up with whatever odd jobs he could find — mowing lawns, raking leaves, weeding gardens, running a paper route, and the like. He had never had a chance to turn out for sports. He often saw the crews rowing on Lake Union while he was out working and gradually was filled

---

[2] The Grand Coulee Dam is a concrete gravity dam on the Columbia River in the U.S. state of Washington, built to produce hydroelectric power and provide irrigation water. Constructed between 1933 and 1942.

with a fierce determination that one day he would row in one of those shells. When he finally had enough money saved to cover a year's tuition, he enrolled at the University and headed for the shell house.

The other five boys were spread throughout Western Washington.

In seat #3 was Gordy Adam. He grew up on a dairy farm in the small town of Everson, near the Canadian border. He had attended a two-room schoolhouse and then a more modern high school in nearby Deming where he played football. He had to spend five months salmon fishing in the brutal waters off the Alaskan coast to earn money to start at the University. Once on campus, he tried out for football as a walk on, but quickly realized that college level football was not the same animal as small town football, and he would get nowhere. So he tried out for crew. It was, as he would later say, a very good fit.

At stroke was Don Hume. He hailed from Anacortes — a lumber town and fishing port 50 miles north of Seattle. When his father lost his job at the lumber mill and the family moved to Olympia in search of work, Don stayed with family friends to finish high school. After graduation, he worked for a year at the pulp mills, but when his job gave out he took a rowboat he had found and refurbished and rowed the roughly 100 miles to his family in Olympia — a six-day trip. In the fall he registered at the University.

In seat #7 was my Dad, Joe Rantz. Joe was listed as a Seattle boy by the University and in news publications, because he graduated from Roosevelt High in Seattle, but his heart and the only place that had ever felt like home to him were out on the Olympic Peninsula, in Sequim. For much of his life hard work to survive on his own had been his lot. He had taken a year after high school, working back in Sequim, to earn enough money to put himself through the first year of college — and I suppose it didn't hurt that his fiancé, my Mom, was also in Sequim finishing up her senior year. So by the fall of 1933, when both he and my Mom enrolled at the University, he was well muscled and hungry for whatever life had to offer.

In seat #6 was Shorty Hunt. Shorty skipped two years of high school, graduating from the small farming community of Puyallup at age 16. Already 6'3" and an exceptional athlete, he enrolled at the University that fall, the youngest to make the crew. The youngest each year he was on the team, Shorty celebrated his 19th birthday on the day of Opening Ceremonies at the Olympics.

The coxswain was Bob Moch. The only senior in the boat, Bob had grown up in Montesano, a small logging town in the southwestern corner of the State. His father was the town jeweler and watchmaker. Bob was a small, asthmatic kid who topped out at 5'7", but he never let that get in his way. If he got knocked down, he picked himself back up. In high school he lettered in — wait for it — basketball! His father never revealed his Jewish heritage to him until a few days before he left for Germany.

They were a young crew those boys. Of the eight oarsmen, pitted against the best in the world, five were Juniors and three were only Sophomores.

Many people who have read and loved The Boys in the Boat have commented that they wish there was more to read. So, I'm going to tell you some stories that didn't make it into the book and some stories of "life after rowing."

It is perhaps easy to dismiss whatever positive influences Harry, Joe's Dad, had on his life, but they were there. At one point in Sequim, Joe found a bee tree. He rushed back to his father all excited to cut the tree down and get the honey. But Harry told him they needed to wait. That everything had its own timing and the tree shouldn't come down until fall when the bees had made all the honey possible for the year. Patience and timing — those things stuck with Joe.

Again in Sequim when Joe was about 13, he was practicing tuning up the family car fiddling with the carburetor in the '26 Franklin, when something flipped over or dropped off and the engine began racing uncontrollably. Joe was frantic! He couldn't fix the problem no matter what he tried to do. He was sure the engine was going to explode and it would be his fault! In the meantime, his father calmly walked out of the shop, leaned in through the window and turned off the ignition key. Another lesson that stuck with Joe. Don't look for the answer in just one place, think outside the box.

One time at the Gold and Ruby mine, Harry was talking to Joe about the problem of sawdust building up outside the mill. Joe would have been about nine, and I'm sure his father was encouraging him to think about creative solutions to problems. Joe's suggested solution was to use one of the high powered mining hoses and wash the sawdust down into Boulder Creek. Harry let him try it. Apparently it worked pretty slick, although if the Environmental Protection Agency had been around in the '20s, they might have had a problem with it.

And in reality, although Dad had been abandoned in Sequim, he wasn't alone. For almost any venture he set out on, Harry Secor was by his side. His partner in the hayfields. His partner in the not-quite-legal endeavors like the gaffing of salmon and exchanging the liquor a bootlegger left with dandelion wine of their own making. And, when there was haying to be done, Dad and Harry could count on work because they were the best haying team in the valley.

When it wasn't haying season, Charlie McDonald's family opened their doors. Dad would work with Charlie felling and preparing giant cottonwood trees for the pulp mills in exchange for evening meals. One of his most poignant memories was when he one day ran across a large amount of watercress in a stream. He brought it to Charlie's wife, Pearl, and asked her if she'd like to use it for a salad. Dad said it really choked him up that not only did she take the watercress gladly and serve some of it for dinner that night, but she took a large tub filled with water down to the irrigation ditch and put the rest of the watercress into the tub, keeping it moist and cool for several more nights salads. For as often as he had been exiled, scorned or rejected, the simple act of valuing something he had offered touched him deeply.

And of course, always in his corner was my Mom — Joyce Simdars. No matter his circumstances she always stood by him.

Which brings me to memories of music and dancing in Sequim. As you may remember, my grandmother went along on all Mom and Dad's dates while they were in Sequim. Often things would go a little askew. There was the night the lights quit in the Franklin and Mom had to stand on the running board holding a flashlight while Dad drove. There was the night the car quit partway home and Grandma and Mom had to push while Dad steered — what!? I guess neither of them knew how to steer a car. There was the time the Franklin refused to start after a dance and they all had to walk home in the freezing weather, Dad carrying his banjo and Mom in her dancing shoes with Grandma trudging along behind.

The dance I would love to have seen was the night Dad got carried away with his irreverent sense of humor. As usual he was in the band for the first half of the dance to earn admission to the second half. As he was singing "Shine on Harvest Moon", for some reason he felt compelled to alter the chorus — which is supposed to go like this:

"Shine on, shine on harvest moon up in the sky,
I ain't had no lovin 'since January, February, June or July."

But, knowing absolutely where Mom was in the crowd, he sang it like this:

"Shine on, shine on harvest moon up in the sky,
I ain't had no lovin " '(pauses, grinning meaningfully at Joyce)
 "... much ... since January, February, June or July ."

Well Mom went beet red, alternately mortified and laughing. The crowd on the dance floor hooted. I asked her if she let him dance with her after that — she said "of course." I never heard what Grandma thought.

People often ask "What was your Dad like as a father? I think that can best be illustrated by examples:

When we were small, Seattle used to get a lot more snow. And as soon as a snow storm hit Dad would haul all the "kid sleds" down from the crawl space above the garage. But what we really waited for was Saturday, because if the snow held, Dad would get out the bobsled.

This was a huge old homemade contraption with a wooden seat about eight feet long and mounted on two sets of wide wooden runners which would go over pretty much any kind of snow. The runners in the back were fixed, and the runners in the front could rotate for steering. Dad would sit in the front and jam his feet onto the back of those rotating runners and could steer by straightening one leg or the other. For those of us who were piled on behind, we would either hang on for dear life to the person in front of us or grab the handrails beside the seat.

There was a spectacular snowstorm in January of 1950 and over the weekend we practically ran the runners off that bobsled. My brother Fred and I were eight and six that winter. My little brother Jerry was almost two and spent most of his time in a box either being pulled or riding in front of one of us on our little sleds. When Dad took the bobsled down the hills we had Jerry-in-the-box wedged between Dad's knees and us kids behind him.

But this particular storm dropped enough snow that Dad had a really *"Great and Exciting Idea"*. Perkins Way, in Lake Forest Park, was a narrow, continuously winding road which had a steady downhill slope for about a mile. Dad had to drive the car, towing the bobsled, but first thing you know, there we were, poised at the top of Perkins Way. Mom put her foot down about Jerry-in-the-box taking the ride, but for the rest of us, with Dad in the front and a pile of us behind him, we were ready for the thrill of our lives.

Down the hill we started, with the bobsled steadily picking up speed. As we went whizzing down through the curves we started to hear an eerie rumbling sound, which grew louder and louder as we went faster, until it seemed that our world consisted of nothing but that sound and the wind. Our hair was flying back, our noses were freezing, our eyes were tearing up and everything was just a blur! And when we coasted to a stop at the end of the hill, we knew that never, ever, in our lives would we EVER do anything that exciting again — and we didn't. I don't recall that Dad ever took that bobsled down Perkins Way again. I suspect that Mom might have had something to do with that, too.

One of the things Dad would do for our birthdays when we were kids was to create a sort of "scavenger hunt" for our birthday present. He would wrap and hide a present, and then write a series of age-appropriate poems, each one a clue that led you to the next clue and eventually to your present, which might have been in the oven or up in the attic, or maybe out in the garage.

When I got into high school, through a series of odd events, I wound up with an unbroken six-month old horse. Not knowing the least thing about horse training, I immediately joined a 4-H club and got several books on how to train a horse.[3] One of the books touted the benefits of teaching your horse to pull a cart, because it could be done while the horse was still too young to ride. Of course I promptly showed Dad a picture of a horse hitched to a training cart and said "I need one of these to do the job right." I never thought about how he would do it, but not much time passed before an amazing replica of a training cart made with plumbing pipes and elbows, lightweight motorcycle wheels, and various hand carved wood pieces appeared.

It turned out that my horse disliked pulling anything, and often would go on bucking sprees which made short work of the wooden shaft poles. However, Dad was up to the challenge, and there progressively appeared an ever larger pile of replacement shafts for

---

[3] The 4-H stands for Head, Heart, Hands, and Health. At 4-H club meetings members recite the Pledge of Allegiance: I pledge my Head to clearer thinking, my Heart to greater loyalty, my Hands to larger service, and my Health to better living, for my club, my community, my country, and my world.

whenever I came leading the horse home with the busted cart dragging behind us. He never complained, he'd just shake his head and replace the shafts.

That's the kind of Dad he was. Someone adventurous, creative, patient and unfailingly supportive of our passions.

When I graduated from the University of Washington, class of '65, I landed a job at Boeing.

As it happened Dad also worked at Boeing and my job was at the same plant he was working in, so I could ride in his carpool. Dad had always had a carpool that he drove for as long as I can remember and many of his riders stayed with him for their entire time at the company. One of those riders was a lady named Shirley.

Shirley was a formidable looking single lady, with a distinctive Brooklyn accent, who lived with her mother. I suppose she wasn't more than 40 at the time, but to a girl of 21 she seemed a lot older than that. And she had one real weakness. She couldn't resist betting with Dad. Could not! No matter how stupid the subject. Dad had a can on the car floor that he had punched a slotted hole into — a Metracal can I think — that any time he won a bet with Shirley she had to pony up a quarter. I'm not sure what he ever did with that money.

She would bet on anything. A car was driving slowly in front of us and she would say something like, "Probably an old man with a pipe." Dad would say, "I think it's a woman." She would say, "Wanna bet?" Dad would say, "You're on," and work his way up beside the car. Well, it was never the old man with the pipe, so out would come the quarter. Ka-ching.

She would say, "It's cloudy everywhere today." He would say, "Probably not cloudy over Sequim." She would say, "Wanna bet?" He would say, "You're on." Eventually we would get far enough south that we could see the skyline over the Olympic Peninsula. Ka-ching. As I said, she could not resist.

I never saw her win a bet — except that once.

But the real classic, the one I always think of when the month of May comes around, happened about midway through the month. The weather had been cold and miserable and hardly a day passed that it hadn't rained. One morning Shirley grumbled her way into the car and said, "It's never going to warm up." Dad, "Oh, it'll hit 90 before the end of the month." Shirley, "Wanna bet?" Dad, "You're on." Well, the days dragged past. Cold days, wet days, and even if the sun peeked out for a while we never got up to 70. Finally came the end of the last week. May 31st was on a Sunday, so on Friday 29th, Shirley got into the car smiling; Dad graciously handed her a 50-cent piece. I thought it was over. He had never flinched, but he had lost the bet.

However, through some anomaly of nature, Sunday the 31st dawned clear and the temperature shot up and surpassed 90 degrees! The next day, when Dad pulled up at her driveway, Shirley came flouncing out of her house, slammed her body into the car, shoved a silver dollar into the Metracal can and loudly said, "It'll be a cold day in May before I ever bet with you again!"[4] Dad's face remained absolutely straight as he eased the car out of her driveway, but I could almost see the thought balloon forming over his head…"Wanna bet?"

In looking back on Dad's life, something people often ask about is "Did being an Olympic Medal winner change his life?" That's not really the right question. The right question is "Did being on crew change his life?" and the answer to that is "Yes, profoundly". He came into the University a damaged soul, unable to trust, and he left a whole person.

What may seem odd to us now, when getting Olympic Gold can garner you quite a tidy living in awards and sponsorship opportunities, is that none of the guys wanted that. They were ferociously protective of their status as amateurs. In those days one of the major opportunities for money and fame was — believe it or not — to get

---

[4] Metracal was a brand of diet foods introduced in the early 1960s.

your face on the Wheaties cereal box. "Wheaties, the Breakfast of Champions."

The guys were approached by General Mills and to a man they turned the offer down. They were a very humble group of guys. They put the Gold Medals away. They walked away from the University. They walked away from rowing. They built lives and families for themselves, but they never could walk away from the crew. Because their bonding as a crew was in their blood. At least twice a year for the rest of their lives they would gather together. Sometimes with families, sometimes just them. And every 10 years they celebrated with an anniversary row in the Husky Clipper.

I have to say that, of all the accolades Dad received from rowing, for him the most important recognition was induction into the inaugural class of the Husky Hall of Fame. That purple jacket represented the ultimate affirmation of his value to the University — his value to the crew.

Which is not to say that being a Gold Medal winner doesn't have its perks. When Mom died in 2002, I was ordering the engraving on the marble piece for the niche wall where we would be placing her ashes in Sequim. The representative explained to me that it would make sense to also put all of Dad's information, except the date of death, on at the same time. I requested that after Mom's dates there be etched a small rhododendron. "Oh no," the representative on the phone said, "we don't allow anything but names and dates on the niche walls." "Well," I said, "what about if after everything is engraved I just come and paint a small rhody beside the dates?" "Oh no," he said, "we can't have any color. It would make things too messy." "Well," I said, thinking frantically, "that's really too bad, because my Dad is probably the only Gold Medalist Sequim ever had and I had wanted to put the Olympic Rings after his name." Long pause. "What's your phone number? I'll call you back in a few minutes." About five minutes later, the phone rang and the representative's voice asked, "What did you say the colors on those rings were?" And I said, "Does this mean my Mom gets her rhododendron?" Dad may have been humble, but I was never above name dropping.

And so, on June 4th of 2013, The Boys in the Boat was released and we held our collective breath. We didn't know. Everyone who had read the manuscripts and raved about them was also someone already prejudiced toward the story. How would it be received by people who had never even known this had happened?

We were blown away!

The book began to take on a life of its own. People laughed and wept. They read the race scenes on the edge of their seats. And when the book was over many felt a disquieting emptiness — as though they had been at a great party with friends and the whole scene just evaporated. Some found it hard to read another book for a while. Many needed to reread the book or just think about it to process the journey they had completed. And most felt they had been given a gift — a gift that it was important to share.

I have been trying to figure out what it is about The Boys in the Boat that effects people so deeply.

There is, first of all, the fact that on its own it is just a great story. It's a great sports story, a great human-interest story. It's got survival struggles, underdogs, a likeable "hero", insurmountable obstacles, self-doubt, and finally supreme trust and victory. And through it all the central character just keeps trudging on, conquering his world one step at a time.

Second, it is the story of rowing. For those who dedicate their lives to the pain and the beauty of this sport it validates their passion. It explains like no other book what it is to row — what it takes to be a rower. People who row can give this book to their non-rowing friends and say, "Read this. This is why I do it. This is what it's like." People who know someone who rows can say, "I wish I had read this before. Now I see. Now I understand."

Third, it is a true story. One of the recurring themes we notice in the reviews is that if this weren't a true story it would have lost people's interest because it was too improbable to happen. And yet it did. And because of that, people have stopped to take a look at their own circumstances. "If Joe could do that — maybe I could do this." "Maybe things aren't as tough as I thought." "Maybe there's a light at the end of the tunnel." "Maybe I could learn to row — reconnect with my old friends — take music lessons — take a step into the unknown." The story has become a source of inspiration — even courage — to many people.

But something that lies even deeper than the truth of the story is its unflinching probing into the human condition. Even if we don't recognize it at a conscious level, somewhere deep down the truth of what is important to us as humans vibrates throughout our souls. And the book lets us stop and take a look deep down and remember what things in life are really important. We see trust and sacrifice and longing for home, and love and suffering and redemption and honor and grief and joy, and our hearts swell and tears come to our eyes because those things lie at the heart of what it is to be human.

I expect that maybe the reason the response to the book has been so intense is that in this age of "me-first-its-all-your-fault-you're-wasting-my-time-I-can't-get-everything-done-I-can't-get-anything-done-when-can-I-breathe??" this may be the first time many people have ever touched those feelings. And it startles them. And it washes over them. And they realize that they have just experienced something important, even if they don't fully understand it. Because, what they have experienced is a look into what we can be like when we are at our best. And it changes them.

Kind of like it changed Dad, I guess.

Because, in the end, the boy who had been totally disposable to his family, the boy who had vowed never to trust again, found a home. I once asked Dad why he kept coming back to crew and to all that pain and crushing effort. I expected him to say it was because he needed the job the University provided for crew members. But that's not what he said. What he said was simply, "**They needed me.**"

Gloria DiFulvio

Gloria DiFulvio contacted me after I posted a request for Rowing Tales contributions on the Masters Rowing International Facebook Group. This is one of two Tales she's contributed to this book. The story relates to the balance between pain caused by rowing and the deep satisfaction of the outcomes of rowing training. Most of us reading this can empathise and respond with our own versions of this tale.

At Home On The Water

My alarm rings: 4:11am. I pry myself from my pillow. Eyes barely open. The moon and stars still high in the sky. Morning sun tucked behind the tree-lined river. My body hurts. I attempt to soothe it, by stretching. Maybe throw a yoga child's pose in for good measure. Because that will not be enough, I pop two Advil keeping the soreness at bay. I'm a rower. Pain is part of my day.

My partner and I are in this together. Arriving at the boathouse, we're greeted by the familiar chatter of our teammates doing what they do - carrying oars to the water, gas to the safety launches. We join in doing our part. All for each other. We are ready to row.

Eight women carry the boat to the river and place it in the glassy water. The sun welcomes us, peeking out over the hills into a bright pink sky.

I am home.

With a healthy fear of water, this is the last place I expect to find myself. But it's where I belong. A quiet ease takes over as I sit with my teammate's oar in hands. We propel ourselves down the river, fight fatigue, welcome sweat, feel our strength, commit to one another. The eagle watches us from his perch on the oak. I see him take flight alongside us and wonder if joining our crew is part of his routine too.

Lawrence Fogelberg

Lawrence is an American abroad - he learned to row at Phillips Exeter Academy where senior members of the crew were allowed to use the skiffs belonging to the school's principal and teachers. He continued to row while a student at Harvard University. While at university, he raced and won the 1965 Lightweight Singles event in the first year of the Head of the Charles Regatta. Realising that the fiftieth anniversary was due in 2014, he was determined to return and race his single again - this time in the Men's Senior Veterans over 70 year age category. This Rowing Tale is a record of his correspondence with the HOCR administration and so many helpful fellow rowers who enabled him to take part. Lawrence came 32nd out of 50. He now lives in Germany.

Reliving Past Glories

21st March, 2014
[To HOCR Administration]

Greetings!

What do I have to do to qualify for the Senior-Veteran Singles MEN (70+)?

I am the L. Fogelberg who won the HOCR Lt.Wt. Men's Single in 1965. I am still actively rowing, for 30+ years now with the Frankfurter Rudergesellschaft Germania in Germany.

http://www.frg-germania.de/

In the last few years, I was in the crew of FRG eights. I also scull, of course.

I have not competed in similar singles events here for my age group. Looking at the 2013 results for Senior-Veteran Singles, I am confident, however, that I wouldn't be last, also not first.

Still a US citizen, I obviously cannot meet the 75% non-US crew requirement for the International Entry Application. Can this be winked at? Also, there are no regattas over here before May 1st with a race for seniors in which I could compete to document my time. What about an affidavit from my club, target, less than 30 minutes?

So, what chance do I have to qualify for the event, a nostalgia bonus as a winning competitor in the first HOC Regatta?

Thank you for your attention. Looking forward to hearing from you.

Sincerely,
Larry Fogelberg. H '66

7th April, 2014
[To L. Fogelberg]

Hi Larry

Thank you for your email. Following inquiries from a few of our 1965 competitors interested in returning this year, the Managing Directors have decided to make a limited number of entries available to crews or athletes who raced in the first HOCR.

At this point, they are planning to notify accepted crews by mid-May. Please let me know if the mid-May notification deadline would pose an issue for you to make your travel arrangements.

If you have any questions, please let me know. We very much hope to see you in October!

Best,
Kate Broderick
Director of Operations, Head Of The Charles Regatta

8th April, 2014
[To HOCR Administration]

Hi Kate,

Many thanks for your reply. Living overseas, the earliest possible notification would be appreciated, but mid-May would also be fine.

Hoping for the best!

Regards,
Larry Fogelberg

20th May, 2014
[To L. Fogelberg]

Dear Larry

I am pleased to inform you that our Rules Directors have agreed to guarantee your entry to the Men's Senior-Veteran 1x. We are very excited to have you join us as one of the athletes who competed in the first Head Of The Charles.

You will need to submit your entry online. Registration will open in the second week of June, so please check back on our website then.

Please let me know if you have any other questions. We look forward to seeing you in October!

Best,
Kate Broderick

20th May, 2014
[To HOCR Administration]

Mmmm! "Kuss die Hand!" Austrians would say as a heartfelt thanks.

I'll do everything I can to be there.

Best regards,
Larry

And so now to make the arrangements for boat and accommodation.

20th May, 2014
[To the Master of Eliot House and his wife][5]

Greetings to both of you. I have a very wild request.

I (H 66) rowed for Eliot House fifty years ago, also in the crew that went to Henley in 1965 to defend the Thames Challenge Cup, which the Eliot crew had won the previous year. As a lightweight sculler, I won the first Head of the Charles regatta in 1965. The regatta rules directors have guaranteed my entry to the 50th regatta this year.

My request: Is there an outside chance that Eliot House has a guest room I could occupy the two weeks preceding the regatta?

Of course, I would pay something, guided by what I see for B&B accommodations in Cambridge, more for the pleasure of meals, very open to negotiation.

If you needed an "excuse" for my presence, I would happily host a couple of sherry evenings to talk with students. (Do they still exist, as they did in John Finley's day?)

I wasn't much of a scholar, went to Citibank with my BA, and have lived in Germany ever since. It wouldn't be like meeting Ted Kennedy, as I did, but maybe the students would be interested in

---

[5] Eliot is one of the residential 'Houses' or halls of residence for students at Harvard University. The shorthand Harvard graduates use to describe themselves by the year of their graduation, Larry is H 66 meaning he graduated from Harvard in 1966. John H. Finley Jr was a Professor of Classics at Harvard and Master of Eliot House from 1941 - 1968. Ted Kennedy was a politician representing Massachusetts US Senator for 46 years. presidential candidate and brother of President John F. Kennedy.

hearing about "back when," working abroad, a German view of European and US politics. Questions lead to discussion.

Any chance?

Hoping, sincerely,
Larry Fogelberg

21st May, 2014
[To L. Fogelberg]

Dear Larry,

We would be delighted to have you stay in Eliot. We have the Matthiessen Suite, which is our guest room, and as it is in the heart of the undergrad housing, will give you the full experience of Eliot House life.

I am cc'ing our House Administrator, who will put you on the calendar for that time. She will be your contact person for all sorts of things during your time here - she runs the place!

Doug and I look forward to meeting you, and hearing about your time in the House.

All best,
Gail O'Keefe

21st May, 2014
[To Gail O'Keefe, Eliot House]

Oh my gosh!

It's raining roses on my plans! Thank you, and for replying so soon. I hardly slept last night, wondering if I would really be able to organize things for this nostalgic trip back to Cambridge and Harvard. Wow!

Thank you both again,

Best regards,
Larry

Now to organise a boat.

20th May, 2014
[To Dan Boyne in charge of Weld Boathouse][6]

Greetings, Dan Boyne!

First, who am I: a grad, H 66; now recreational sculler, winner of the lightweight singles at the first Head of the Charles. I have been guaranteed entry in the Men's Senior-Veteran 1x this year.

Wow! They're letting me come back for the fiftieth HOCR!

---

[6] Dan Boyne is a rower, author and coach writing about rowing and fitness topics. Weld is one of two boathouses used by Harvard University rowing crews.

I need a boat, any boat for my 80 kg, 176 lb. I won back then in a Weld Boathouse boat, it wasn't the lightest skiff in the race. I am not going to win, so that is not important.

What chance do I have to use a boat from your boathouse?

I want to train for a week or two on the Charles. It wouldn't have to be a boat reserved for me, any one for my weight available, and my "training" times would be flexible, whenever there was less demand.

AND, of course, I would pay whatever is necessary - well, almost. I expect that there is a membership fee for grads.

So, what are my chances? Anything else you need to know?

Best regards,
Larry Fogelberg

21st May, 2014
[To L. Fogelberg]

Dear Larry,

I would be happy to help you with a boat. Just circle back a few weeks before the regatta to remind me/confirm that you are coming.

Best,
db (Dan Boyne)

21st May, 2014
[To Dan Boyne]

Dear Dan,

Wow, thanks! Before I wrote you, I asked the masters of Eliot House if there was a possibility of using a guest room (I rowed at Henley for Eliot back then). Before I got up this morning, I had a message that I could.

My good luck is almost too good to believe: in 24 hours all logistic problems solved.

You will hear from me, and I am looking forward to meeting you.

Thanks again and all the best,
Larry

26th July, 2014
[To L. Fogelberg from HOCR administration]

Lawrence Fogelberg,

The following application has been received for the 2014 Head of the Charles Regatta:

Event 1: Men's Senior Veteran Singles I and II [70+] Application#1680

Affiliation(s) Unaffiliated (GER)

1st August, 2014
[To L. Fogelberg from HOCR administration]

Dear Lawrence Fogelberg (Frankfurter Rudergesellschaft Germania),

Congratulations on your acceptance into the Men's Senior Veteran Singles I and II [70+] for L. Fogelberg at the 2014 Head Of The Charles® Regatta.

We look forward to having you at the 50th edition of America's Fall Rowing Festival!

8th September, 2014
[To L. Fogelberg]

Mr. Fogelberg,

Kate Broderick at the Head of the Charles office gave me your name. I am writing an article on the 1965 Regatta for this year's program, and I'm hoping I might have the chance to talk with you about your experiences. If you are by chance local to the Boston area, I'd love to buy you coffee or lunch, and if you're farther afield, perhaps we could have a phone conversation?

Thanks for your time. Hope we have the chance to talk soon.
Chuck Fountain

9th September, 2014
[To Charles Fountain]

Mr. Fountain,

I will be in Cambridge for the regatta, as Kate confirmed. I will be staying in Eliot House from Oct. 6 to 20, "training", using a single from Weld Boathouse.

You can imagine how lucky I am that Harvard is being sooo hospitable.

Who is the article for?

Perhaps you can jog my memory with a few questions to help me "search the files in my head."

I rowed for Eliot House in 1965, trying to defend the Henley Royal Regatta Thames Challenge Cup, which the 1964 crew won. We couldn't, but pushed Isis (Oxford Univ. 2nd boat) to a new course record in the semifinal.

When I returned to Harvard after an academically forced leave of absence, I probably got into Eliot House by the chance that I spoke to John Finley just when he was opening the case with the Henley trophy, and could tell him that I had seen them win and that I had an lightweight "H" from my sophomore year.

Probably should have been put on probation, but that would precluded my staying on the Univ. squad!

Let me know. Regards,
Larry Fogelberg

10th September, 2014
[To L. Fogelberg]

Larry,

Thanks so much for getting back to me. I teach at Northeastern. I probably should have mentioned that every year I take a team of my journalism students and we write (they write, I edit) news and feature stories for the Regatta website.

Attached is what we did with last year's Regatta:

Anyway this story is one I'm writing myself, and it will appear in the official Regatta program. It's going to be, I hope, a full story on the planning and execution of the first regatta in 1965.

I'd like to ask you about whatever you remember about that first HOCR, how you first heard about it, what you knew about head racing, what you remember about the experience or the race itself. My deadline is going to be in advance of your arrival in Boston, I'm afraid. Perhaps we could talk on the phone sometime before that?

Look forward to talking to you, and hope we might have the chance to meet during Regatta weekend.

Chuck Fountain

10th September, 2014
[To Charles Fountain]

Chuck,

Sounds good. I cannot remember anything about the founding and organization of the HOCR.

After Henley, I was at H summer school making up a couple of credits and sculling. When we heard of the regatta, Paul Wilson and I registered. Paul was stroke of the Eliot House crew both years at Henley.

I do remember that the timing was a little less professional than the first program suggests when it says: "Computer Assisted Timing by IBM".

Someone I knew was involved with the timing team. There was a clock at the start and finish lines (kitchen-style wall clock). At the awards reception in the evening, he told me that they discovered that the sweep second hand "dragged" from 6 to 12, catching up from 12 to 6, and that they adjusted times accordingly - only a few seconds!

But maybe you don't want to mention something like that. (IBM? A spreadsheet to record times and calculate course times? Quite an achievement back then.)

I had heard of "head" races and bumping races - when, where? Maybe when at Henley 1964, on leave from the US Army in Germany, or in 1965.

Recollections of the race itself? None really. I just did my thing, very familiar with the course, no steering problems. I joke that I won because of that, but my course record time, which was better than that of the Senior Championship Singles, stood for a couple of years. I should give credit to Joe Brown, H ´53 (Harald O. J. Brown), coach of the Eliot House crews, who introduced us to the rowing style and training Karl Adam developed that made German crews champions back then: high stroking, interval training.

Yes, give me a call. Maybe your questions will jog some other recollections.

Looking forward,

Larry

10th September, 2014
[To L. Fogelberg]

Larry:

Thanks for all this. I will try to call you tomorrow morning Boston time. Looking forward to it.

Chuck

11th September, 2014
[To L. Fogelberg]

Chuck,

Great talking with you. I'm looking for photos.

Here is a wicked one, taken after the turn of the 12 km Roseninselachter regatta: "Verdammt! Still another 20+ minutes to the finish line!" We won in our age classification.

I will be rowing for Frankfurter Rudergesellschaft Germania 1869 e.V. Several years ago, a young eight from here came in 2nd at the HROC, registered as FRG Germania. Another one just won the Thames Challenge Cup at Henley this year. I have been a member since 1980 or '81.

In 1966 I won the NRA 150 lb. Singles in Philadelphia, and in 1972 was no. 2 in an eight from Mosman Rowing Club that won the Ladies Challenge Cup at the Australian Henley in Melbourne.

As a soldier, I was a member of the Wassersportverein Schifferclub Neckarrems and then of the Mannheimer Ruder-Club von 1875 e.V.

From 1966-68 I was a member of the Ruder-Club "Allemannia von 1866". Yeah, that is the official name.

Hope I get a better photo for you.

Got to go and hope the water isn't too rough,
Larry

11th September, 2014
[To Charles Fountain]

Chuck,

More photos than you wanted, and six more with another email. In the other set, there is one of me wearing a Bavarian jacket and my club cap, which I will be wearing at the HOCR (not the jacket; gave to our son-in-law, since they are now living in Munich).

If a photo is used, it would be very nice if Jochen Blum were credited as photographer.

Cheers,
Larry

11th September, 2014
[To Charles Fountain]

Here is the set with the Bavarian jacket, a nice reference to my living in Germany and the Roseninsel regatta, and the cap as an identifier on race days.

But it's all up to you and the person doing layout.

And again, it would be very nice if Jochen Blum were given credit. He is a great oarsman, stroke, but suddenly had a burst artery or major vein, and has to live with the fear that it could happen again.

Enough. Thank you for your interest. I have to find out if my cellphone will work in the States. You should be able to contact me through the administrator of Eliot House, Sue Weltman.

All the best,
Larry

9th October, 2014
[To L. Fogelberg]

Larry:

I'm glad that you are settling in to some training on the Charles. You are one of many guests and other regular denizens of the boathouse, so please keep in mind the following:

Try not to wander into the coaches offices or practices--they are working!

We do not have public computers at Weld.

Cell phone use should be done outside the boathouse.

Saturdays we are open 6:30-10 am for sculling.

Sunday we are closed.

Best,
db

17th October, 2014
[To L. Fogelberg]

Hi Lawrence,

My name is Eva Maldonado, and I am a journalism student at Northeastern University. I am working for the press for the Head of the Charles, and I would like to know if you are interested in meeting with me for an interview about the regatta and your experience with it through the years. I am available to talk with you at the race whatever time and day best suits you, so please let me know.

Best,
Eva Maldonado

19th October, 2014
[To L. Fogelberg]

Hi Larry,

Just wanted to let you know I'll be there tomorrow after your race, I'll look for you and see if there's some time for us to talk for the press.

Thanks so much!
Eva

Eva was there in Weld, when I returned after the race.

27th October, 2014
[To Eva Maldonado]

Hi Eva,

A bit late to reply. My cell phone didn't work in USA, but you found me and wrote a very nice interview. Was I ever surprised and delighted to find it a couple of days ago! First one on the HOCR website, thank you! That and Fountain's mention of me in the program made the trip and my not-so-successful effort a success for me. (Good thing that I remembered to thank the organization for letting me row, so that the interview didn't end with the remark about beer.)

All the best with your further studies,
Larry

Author's note: The remark about beer: Eva's last question had been what I thought was the best part of the race. "The first beer after it," I had replied with a grin, at about 9:30 in the morning!

My race had been as good as I could hope, starting with number 45 (of 50) on my back, finishing 37th. I didn't pass all those old guys; a few earlier starters must have faded but crossed the finish line ahead of me. I was chagrined, however, that number 46 passed me under the railroad bridge a couple of hundred yards after the start as did 47. I knew number 44 from Union Boat Club would disappear; he had been in the Eliot House crew with me in 1965, racing for Riverside Boat Club over the decades, just never in a single, hence his high starting number. All three finished in the teens. No one else passed me – I believe – so I was happy. Hey, my time was only 5 minutes above what it had been 50 years before – umm, well, 25% higher.

27th October, 2014
[To the Weld Boathouse manager and women's coach]

Dan and Liz,

I missed the email from Dan about not wandering into the coaches' offices, but did, only to thank you both for letting me use a boat and to "train". If I got faster, it was probably from learning to take the curves better. It was a great, nostalgic experience. Thank you both!

That I left Liz´s office with just the cloth hat I have been seeking for years really topped off the whole event. You and your assistants were a great help. All the best for the coming year and more to come.

Best regards, Larry

27th October, 2014
[To L. Fogelberg]

Dear Larry,

So glad to have helped make it memorable! We were excited to see that you did quite well, and the entire Regatta weekend was fabulous. Again, thank you for your generous gift to the house, and the wine, which we will soon be dipping into!

All best regards,
Gail and Doug

27th October, 2014
[To Gail O'Keefe, Eliot House]

Greetings!

You two made my stay in Cambridge, in Eliot House, a high point of my whole visit, meeting you and a few students. In the Matthiesen Suite, I was starting an introduction to the guest book I thought it should have, and then discovered that there already was one - in the closet. Of course! And a delight to read about earlier guests.

My thanks again and all the best to you for this and many coming years,

Larry

2nd November, 2014
[To Charles Fountain]

Hi Chuck,

The interview has delighted family and friends here and USA. I hope you thought it was as good as I did.

Is it possible that you could also excerpt the passages about me in the program text and put them in an email to me?

That would be wonderful. I hope so. Many thanks in advance.

With best regards,
Larry

2nd November, 2014
[To L. Fogelberg]

Larry:

A thousand apologies for not getting back to you last week.
I actually posted the program article to our site when the regatta was over. Here it is:

Thanks so much for all the cooperation you gave. Glad you enjoyed the piece. Glad especially that you had a good return to the Head of the Charles. Hope you get the chance to return again soon.

Chuck

7th November, 2014
[To Charles Fountain]

Chuck,

No apologies! Thank you, that you have replied so soon and for the link to the text. Hope my family and friends can put up with my ego trip - thanks to your interest.
Just a nice fillip to it all for me: for years I have been looking for a Harvard colored cloth-brimmed cap with a green underside of the brim. I had had one, lent it to a friend at the Vogalonga, telling him he could keep it, thinking it wasn't so rare. Then in the window of the Weld office I saw a couple that looked like they might have green under-brims. When I thanked her for Weld's lending me a boat, I asked about the hats with my story. The coach nearest them handed me one: green under-brim. Perfect!

I went back to Eliot and returned and gave her my 2014 T-shirt from the Vogalonga that all participants get. Vogalonga is not a race, and not for single scullers, since the mass start is hectic for coxswains and crews.

Don't bother to reply. I am still on a high from the 2014 HOCR, thanks to your having made it more special for me.

Best regards,
Larry.

Rebecca Caroe

A rower and coach living in Auckland New Zealand and the editor of this book, Rebecca enjoys finding ways to connect rowers from around the world. She hosts the RowingChat podcast and is a moderator in the Masters Rowing International Facebook group. This tale is transcribed from a podcast recording by Johnnie Moore whose exploration of "Unhurried" is about realising our potential for learning and growth.

Unhurried Moments On The Water

JOHNNIE MOORE: This is the Unhurried Moments Podcast. I'm Johnnie Moore.

I'm collecting these stories from people of moments when time shifts. Or something unexpected happens in their lives.

In this episode, we hear from Rebecca Caroe, an entrepreneur and rowing enthusiast.

REBECCA CAROE: I live in Auckland, New Zealand. I row on a lake that's right in the middle of the city. It's above sea level, and it's about 500 metres from the beach, but it's actually a flooded extinct volcano. And so it has quite steep sides. There are houses, trees, and parks lining the banks.

I was rowing my single scull around the lake one morning before going to work. In many ways, I find rowing on my own to be a moving meditation. It's a repetitive moment; every single stroke is a repeat of the one before. The only variation is whether you decide to take more strokes a minute or push harder or when you have to steer around a corner.

The sun was coming up in the east. As it came up, I was turning around on the far side of the lake and preparing for my final run back to the clubhouse. The sun was just peeking over the top of a house. As I started to row away, it came more fully into view.

An intense ray of that early dawn shone down onto the water's surface. It was directly behind me, and it dazzled me. While I rowed, I lined up the stern of my boat, so it was directly extended into the sunbeam. I lifted my chin and looked up towards the horizon under the peak of my cap, and the sunlight flooded into my field of vision so that I couldn't see anything except this ray of light that I was rowing down all the way back to the boathouse.

JOHNNIE: Many of these episodes have been around moments when relationships with other people have changed. It's nice to get ones like this which are more about – I guess you'd call it – solitude.

I also enjoyed this observation from Rebecca about the particular context in which this moment happened.

REBECCA: Because you're going backwards, you have half a mind being concerned that you're about to row into something that you haven't seen because there's quite a significant blind spot directly in front of you – not that there are many obstacles on the lake, but one of the joys of this was that I was absolutely sure that I could continue the moment for as long as I wanted because I knew I wasn't going to be hitting anything. There was nothing else to concern me.

JOHNNIE: One of the interesting things about all these stories is the tiny details of the context contribute to making the unhurried moment happen.

We, as humans, are obviously not in control of that context, and yet we do play a part. We have influence or agency in making these unhurried moments happen.

Thanks for listening.[7]

---

[7] You can find out more at the website – unhurried.org

Greg Spooner

Greg is a Doctor of Physical Therapy in San Diego, California, USA and online at RowPhysio.com. His four-man crew won the North Atlantic Rowing Race from New York City to Bishop Rock, UK in 2006. They crossed the Atlantic Ocean in 69 days, through tropical storm Alberto.

A Green Glob From The Deep

It was 2:30 in the morning in the middle of the Atlantic Ocean, and we're rowing through the heart of the Gulf Stream. The beauty of the Gulf Stream shows in the middle of the night.

There's so much bioluminescence that the water glows, the moment the oar blades dip in. On the flattest of nights, when there's not a cloud in the sky and no moon, the stars blend right into the ocean and you see the glow of these bioluminescent galaxies below.

This one evening, the seas were whipped up by a recent storm, and it was very rough and uncomfortable rowing. A squall passed overhead and dumped rain on our heads so hard that every drop hurt as it thumped every square inch of our skulls.

We tightened up the gaskets on our coat sleeves, rowed with our elbows high into the air, and suffered for about a half an hour until, all of a sudden, the skies parted as the torrent of fresh rainwater that hit the surface of the ocean calmed the seas almost completely flat.

Dylan and I stopped to take a break. We emptied the water out of our jackets and grabbed a snack. As we recuperate from the recent deluge, this large ominous green glob appears below the boat. It was so massive. It had to be a whale visiting in the night.

Ever so silently, as we gazed down over our port side, this green giant disappeared under our boat, and re-emerged on the starboard side. Our little hairs stood on end.

We very quickly clipped ourselves into the boat in case this giant but gentle beast came and gave us a little nudge.

Just as soon as the green glob appeared, it was gone.

We finished our Oreo snack and laughed and grinned for the remaining half hour of our shift before the next two guys came out – seemingly nonbelievers of our incredible encounter.

William de Laszlo

During his world record ocean row around the British mainland, William told us about a serious moment when the crew got into an argument. As I was taught when I was at sailing school, remember, the sea is safe until you forget that it is dangerous. Any conflict at sea is serious. One in the confined space of an ocean rowing boat, doubly so.

Conflict

We were in the north of Scotland when we were running low on water. In an ocean rowing boat our drinking water is stored in ballast below deck, as each tank is emptied, we refill it with sea water and then use a desalinator to make fresh drinking water for the crew. The desalinator pump stopped working and that could have ended the whole row - without water we couldn't survive. So I had to make a call did we stop, or did we carry on with a smaller water ration per man.

The water pump stopping working was what triggered the conflict, and the reason why the water pump stopped working was because we had very poor weather. One of the team members was brilliant. He was like, "We're going to get to Scotland, and the weather is going to be crap, and it's going to stay crap," and it was.

Ultimately, we just didn't have enough solar power to be able to charge up the battery which ran the pump.

It was an interesting moment in the dynamics of the crew when things were getting tough. We were coming up towards the home straight over the halfway point and I had made a call to ration down water intake because, again, we still had no idea how long the race was going to take.

Although we were way ahead of any expected completion time, we still had no idea how long that final leg of the journey was going to go.

This caused an interesting dynamic within the crew because there was unhappiness around that decision. Admittedly, we had a lot of ballast. We had low levels of redundancy and it got to quite a head where one of the team didn't particularly want to continue rowing anymore without having their say.

I think the important thing that I learnt from that dynamic was communication is so important all the way around. We were rowing three hours on and three hours off during the day, two hours on and two hours off during the night. And I think one of the things that helped us so much as a team to diffuse that situation was having a regular slot every day we always had 15 minutes of downtime where we stopped rowing.

So, during that period, we had one moment every day where we all sat down as a team to discuss our achievements, our differences, discuss issues that we might be having, and that was absolutely crucial in terms of making sure the team gelled together.

As the skipper I realised that there was something going on because, in that 15 minutes, one of the team raised it.

You're making a call and you're making a judgment and then how to diffuse that. Ultimately, it was kind of diffused by two of the members of the team giving up their share. They decided to say, "Oh, fine, I'll almost forego my rations if you guys want to have yours."

That actually deflated the whole thing very quickly because there was this balance. "Okay, fine, we'll crack on." Literally, the day later, the sun comes out, the water pump is working again, and it's all forgotten about.

I reflect back and maybe I made the wrong call. Maybe I was being too cautious and, as I said, we had that Lithium-ion battery that we could have dipped into, but I made the call that we just didn't know how long it was going to take us to get home on that last leg.

Peter Becker

Peter lives in the Northwest of the USA and has been rowing and paddling with community groups and masters athletes for years. He says as the son of a naval architect (who hated outboard motors) "I rowed around and was a "wharf rat" from the age of 6... and I still am."

Pocock And Rowing Physics

We have a former national team member as a coach of the Juniors at our club, Debbie Swinford. She was active in the 1989-90 period when Kris Korznowski was coaching the US Rowing team and I was assisting another one of his rowers in Virginia. The C2 Model B rowing machine was all the rage at the time - but it was still pretty new equipment. And some thought pulling oneself up the slide with ones feet was fast. I'm not sure if Kris did or not, but the idea keeps coming around and still gets discussed today.

I don't think it helps and checkfactor on the ActiveSports monitor unit says it hurts the boat run.

I had the opportunity to compare these "modern" discussions against an expert presentation from ages ago. Make up your own mind about what you think is an effective way to move a rowing boat.

I was actually present in the old Pocock Boathouse in Seattle in 1982 when a physicist from the Princeton Center for Advanced Studies casually drew the physics of rowing formulas on a blackboard for George Pocock.

He then dusted off his hands, got on a seaplane with the rest of us and we went off to a research site (I am also a physical oceanographer...and acoustics expert)!

I still remember his diagramming the momentum transfer as the boat went forward and the rower went up the slide. He highlighted that and noted that if a 190 lb rower (85 kg) went up the slide while a 12 kg boat and rower went forward as a unit, minus skin friction and form drag (which were constants over time) if the rower exceeded the boat speed in the opposite direction it slowed the boat (hence we row with ratio).

My fellow coach says according to Kris Korznowski in the 80s you could pull the boat forward with your feet instead of it checking the boat.

Bryan Volpenhein

Bryan is a two-time US Rowing Male Rower of the Year and three times Olympian - most famously as the stroke of the 2004 Athens Olympic eight. This was the first time in 40 years that the USA had won the Olympic eights event and they also set a World Best Time in the heats.

Bryan told this story while talking to Jake and Lawrence on the Row Show podcast.

Faking Erg Scores

I attribute being any good on the erg to a kid on our team that was a lightweight.

At Ohio State we would post our scores in-between classes on a big chalkboard down at the boat house. You'd have to go down and do it when you had time.

There was a lightweight guy there who was on our team who was super fit. He's a good friend of mine. He was posting 5:56 up there for 2k and was making up his erg scores.

At the time, this was in 1996, that was like a world record by 15 seconds. But I didn't know, I was new to crew.

I had no idea. I was like, "Well, fuck this kid. I got 50 pounds on him or more, I should be able to beat him." I was just like, "Well, I guess I should go that fast".

And I just set out to do it. It took me a couple of years, but I ended up doing it, and I went 5:55 in my junior year at the CRASH-B. That's where I got invited to the next round.

I found out that he was lying after I'd beaten the score.

After I'd beaten it, there was this story that came out in USA Today about basically how he went to the trial camp for the '96 Olympics but then got cut. Later in my career I ended up rowing for Mike Teti who was the lightweight coach at that time.

Mike was like, "Yes, I can never get the guy to come to camp."

Then it all sort of came out in the wash. His 6K time got published in USA Today[8] as the top 6K of the camp at 18:24. Somehow, it got past all the checking. People thought, "That was real or what?"

And it all blew up in this guy's face a little bit, and 20 years down the road, we've made up and it's all restored back and moved full circle which is the beautiful thing about rowing.

You let that kind of stuff go.

---

[8] USA Today is a newspaper.

Noel Donaldson

Coach of multiple Olympic medalists, Noel Donaldson coached the Australian "Oarsome Foursome" to two Olympic gold medals and more recently, the Kiwi Pair to gold in Rio. Drew Ginn rowed in the second Olympiad with the Oarsome Foursome winning a gold in Atlanta 1996. He later raced in a pair with similar Olympic success in Athens 2004 and Beijing 2008.

Cometh The Day

It was late 1995 after the World championships and I was coaching the Australian coxless four. They'd raced in 1995 and come fifth. They hadn't probably done enough work, but it was a good fifth and it was a really good springboard to being Olympic champions the following year. We gave them a few weeks off.

Andrew Cooper, who had been a member of the four who won in 1992, was in the crew. They were back training, and Andrew saw fit to tell me as the coach that he didn't think he could see it through the Olympic campaign and give it his all. He'd spent some time away in the country during the break. He loved his farming. He had had a good time there and tried to get back into training.

In the end, he said, "I'd be letting the guys down. You know, I could do it, but I'm not certain I could put my heart and soul into it and be really honest about it."

To me, that's one of the most courageous decisions of any athlete that I've worked with or that I've ever seen – the ability to know when you're done and to know when you possibly could let your mates down even though you might be out there doing it. You know, 99 percent is not good enough.

Andrew pulled out.

We were then looking for someone who was going to fulfil that spot. He was going to be a bow side rower.

The other three guys had a shortlist about who they thought that actually ought to be. Drew Ginn was on that shortlist of about three different people, but he wasn't number one on the shortlist.

I remember I wanted to talk to him a little bit about it. I wanted to find out how motivated he was for it. And I knew that he was staying in the Australian Institute of Sport residences because he was working the AIS programme at the time.

The guys pointed me to his room. I knocked on the door, expecting to find an athlete just sitting back, reading a book or doing something. But he was pretty much sound asleep and, I'm guessing, reasonably hungover at the particular time.

Anyway, I carried out the discussion to ascertain whether he thought he would be in the four or not.

He told me "Yes, I will be in the four, and we will win a gold medal." That's what he actually told me. I thought, "You cocky so and so, but I like your style."

He'd lived with me a couple of years earlier as a young kid when we had him in Under 23s, so I knew him pretty well. His Dad and I got on pretty well, so we had some background, but I did think he was a bit ahead of himself there, though.

Needless to say, we picked a guy - Richard - who did a good job, but then he got injured. Before you know it, we had Drew in the boat, and he performed exceptionally well at the selection trials, and he got selected.

At the Atlanta Olympic games, before the final, we'd had a bomb alert at our residence where we were actually staying. We had to vacate the premises.

We went to our halfway house and had a bit of time to kill before going on to the regatta course, so I thought it was rather opportune that I might have a conversation with Drew reminding him of that particular day when I went to his room. And I said, "Well, here cometh the day, and here cometh the man. Do you remember the conversation?"

He said, "You didn't need to ask me about it." He said, "It's already on my mind." He knew he'd committed he was going to be in the crew, and he knew also he'd committed that we were going to win, so we only had to really look at one another to acknowledge the conversation.

We both knew that we were on the same page at the same time, even as a young athlete.[9]

---

[9] Noel told this story during an interview :
https://rowing.chat/noel-donaldson/

The Washington Post

This report about Henley Royal Regatta was printed in *The Washington Post* 4th July, 1987.

3 Rowers Penalised At Royal Regatta

Three world rowing champions, West German sculler Peter-Michael Kolbe and British pair Steve Redgrave and Andy Holmes, all won their heats yesterday. Then they were penalized for breaking the rules at the 148th Henley Royal Regatta on the Thames River.

An American crew from Yale was also among the winners.

Holmes and Redgrave erred by rowing back down the river to loud applause after breaking the course record by 12 seconds in the Silver Goblets. Kolbe, who also won through to his semifinal, was seen practicing on the course within three minutes of the start of the afternoon session.

Each will now begin today's racing with one false start to their name, which means they can afford no mistakes, as only two starts are allowed.

Peter Coni, the event chairman, called their behavior part of "the McEnroe Syndrome."[10]

---

[10] John McEnroe is a former world number one tennis star. He won Wimbledon three times and he was famous for his on-court disputes with the line judges and occasional temper tantrums that did not endear him to the staid British press of the era.

"No matter how famous they are, it is still absolutely a matter of safety for people to obey the rules," Coni said. "We are not going to have a repeat of some of the antics we saw in the '60s."

Northeastern University

Peter Coni referred to "antics" in the earlier tale "3 Rowers Penalised". This tale is about the search for a trophy to take home, a speciality of overseas crews visiting a regatta. Its notoriety is maintained with an exhibit in the River and Rowing Museum at Henley on Thames and the delightfully good humoured recollections from the participants.

The detail of the anecdote has been compiled from newspaper stories from the Henley Standard and contemporaneous reports from the Northeastern Huskies website all recounted at a reunion visit to Henley 33 years after the fact.

Henley Helmet Heist

The year was 1973, and the Northeastern University crew, known as The Huskies, travel from Boston to Henley Royal Regatta under the guidance of head coach and Henley-on-Thames native Ernest Arlett. Their two crews were entered in the top event for mens 'eights, the Grand Challenge Cup, as well as the Prince Philip Challenge Cup for coxed fours. The club was getting noticed and doing very well on the water. The trouble was, they were also getting noticed off the water.

The eight defeated Wisconsin in the Grand Challenge Cup semifinal before losing to a strong Russian crew in the final. The four dominated its early rounds eventually winning the Prince Philip Challenge Cup and setting a course record that stood for decades.

Off the river, Northeastern was also getting the attention of locals, but for an entirely different reason. John Maslowski, from the Grand crew had set himself two goals for the trip to England.

"My goals when I left Boston were ... to win the Grand Challenge Cup ... and to bring a policeman's helmet back home."

And so when the crew got knocked out in the final on Henley Sunday, John knew he needed to focus on his other goal. He quickly beat a pathway to the local police station which in those days was located prominently on the corner of Market Place at the top of Henley's High Street. Inside, he spoke to the desk sergeant, John Walker, asking him whether he could buy a helmet.

You can imagine what a hardened British policeman thought of an American student wanting to buy part of their uniform! With a well-worn smile the sergeant told him the only way he could get a helmet was if he could manage to get one off a policeman's head and run like hell.

This was clearly one of those moments when a good sense of humour comes into a policeman's job description, but he was also responsible for sowing the seed of the idea in Maslowski's head, a challenge that had to be heeded.

The target for helmet chicanery was the unsuspecting Peter Smart who was on traffic control duty at the Henley crossroads in the centre of town on 1st July, 1973.

Peter Smart recalled: "Suddenly I had a strange feeling that my bald head was much cooler than before. Then I realised this great big, tall, lanky American crew boy had run off down Duke Street with my helmet."

Dutifully, the copper chased after the thief. Remember at that time the British Police were un-armed except for a truncheon and a whistle - it probably looked rather "Keystone Cops" to on-lookers.

Maslowski later recounted his version of the theft.

"I spotted my 'victim' 50 yards ahead. I walked up behind the officer and snatched his helmet and ran in the opposite direction. The officer blew his whistle and the chase was underway. I remember quite a commotion behind me ... dogs barking, people yelling for me to stop, people jumping out of cars trying to bring me down. I knew I was in TROUBLE. I ended up getting tackled by a young man I later found out was a rugby player. I was handcuffed by the officer and marched back up the main street to the police station where I was put in a room by myself."

Any arrest has to be logged by the desk sergeant and of course, as soon as Smart explained to John Walker why he'd arrested Maslowski, Walker knew it was because of his earlier advice to the American. This provoked a great deal of laughter among the assembled police but not from Peter Smart, the intended victim, who failed to see the funny side.

At this point, the rest of Maslowski's crew mates appeared at the Police Station, clearly they knew about the theft attempt.

"We walked into the station and explained that one of our strong-bodied but weak-minded comrades was being detained. A policeman asked us to sit down and said that he'd be back in a couple of minutes. We were ready to block John's ears for his boneheaded move."

"The sergeant returned with a brown paper bag. He pulled out an old Metropolitan Police uniform helmet and explained that if we promised not to take it out of the bag until we departed the UK, then John could have it."

"I will never forget that extremely kind gesture — EVER." says Maslowski, "I opened the bag and saw MY helmet! It now sits in a cherished spot in my house ... I smile every time I look at it."

In 2006 the parties to the Henley Helmet Heist were reunited. John presented Peter with a specially made helmet trophy declaring that this was to stay with him in Henley until Northeastern University defeats a crew at the Royal Regatta. The helmet was on display at the museum from 2006 and the Americans visited almost every year in order to watch the regatta and see their friend.

The trophy eventually went back to America as a Northeastern crew beat Galatasaray in the Ladies 'Challenge Plate at the 2013 regatta — their first Henley victory since 2006.

CeCe Aguda

CeCe Aguda rows in Puget Sound, Washington State, USA. She started rowing at Johns Hopkins University in 1983 as a charter member of the crew club (it wasn't a varsity sport yet). For 32 years she yearned to return to rowing. Her husband even said that when they watched rowing on TV, he could see her hands twitch. Life had taken her to 9 states and to England, before finally settling on Whidbey Island, 2 hours north of Seattle, Washington, in 2016. One of the first things she did after moving was to read "Boys in the Boat". In 2017 she finally got back in a boat with Whatcom Rowing in Bellingham, and since has rowed with Pocock Rowing Club in Seattle, making the 4 hour round-trip trek two to three times a week to train with a team. The rest of the time she rows her single at home, where she is working to start a club on the island.

Rowing With Whales

A loon yodel echoed in the distance. The staccato whistling of a flock of pigeon guillemot came from behind me as they ran across the water to escape my approach. The rising sun cast a golden carpet across the glassy water, gilding my wake as I glided in my Fluidesign toward the west end of the cove. The low rumble of our motorboat was muffled, as my husband kept pace with me on our joint morning outing. Clunk, plop, swish, clunk.... My oars sang their rhythm against the undertone of the steady hiss of the hull through the water.

POOOFFFF POOOFFFF resounded from across the cove. My head whipped to the right, my oars paused at the release. Two heart-shaped clouds hung above the water as long dark backs slid silently beneath them. Honk honk honk honk!!!! Darryl sounded his horn to make sure I saw them. Two gray whales were casually making their way west, a little to the south of where we were along the north bank.

A brief phone exchange and we turned around to let them travel unhindered. POOOFFFF POOOFFFF they blew again as I watched them continue west.

Ten strokes later I stopped again. More spouts erupted behind the gray whales. Then three tall black fins arced out of the water. Orcas! Another phone exchange. Orcas. Behind you. After a moderate pause to ensure they continued west, we started back to the east (and my car).

About 1000m later I was hailed from the shore. A friend with binoculars asked me if I was watching the orcas. But she pointed east! No, I said, I was rowing away from those 3 to the west. Looking where she pointed, I saw 4-5 more orcas. Darryl – back on the phone – more orcas in front of you.

Slowly we continued east toward my car and the mouth of the cove – Darryl making sure he kept the appropriate regulated distance from the whales. As we neared the boat ramp, he called me again. Will you please get off the water? With 9 to 10 whales in the cove within a mile of me, I was happy to oblige.

Over the next few weeks I had about 5 or 6 more encounters with gray whales in the cove. Easter morning two came feeding in the shallow waters along the north shore, where the muddy bottom is rich with shrimp. I rowed quickly to the shore, where I beached my boat and stood to watch them circle and spin, stirring up shrimp in the mud. Joined by a third, they moved into the little bay where I launch. I waited as they fed until I could get back in my boat and row back to my car.

Several weeks later, most of the whales had supposedly migrated towards their summer waters. Darryl and I again were moving west along the north bank of the cove. I stopped occasionally, thinking I heard something behind me, and kept attributing it to infrequent cars on the west shore. Less than 200m from where I would turn to head south, honk honk honk honk. I stopped. I looked. Nothing. Phone call. What? There's a whale behind you. I looked. Are you sure it's not a seal? (Cue deep sigh from husband) It's a whale. I saw the blow. Poooofffff. A gentle sound, barely audible. Turning, I saw the remnant of a spout as his back slipped beneath the surface, the water sealing behind him and leaving no trace that the 30 to 40 foot whale had ever been there.

Shaken, as were it not for Darryl watching out for me, I would have continued to row right into his path, I watched the whale make his way south close to the western shore. Hoping that he continued to move away, I turned and headed back east.

Am I afraid of a gray whale attacking me?

No, perhaps an orca might, but gray whales feed on shrimp and other small sea creatures. But seen from below in my boat, I look like a log, many of which frequently float through the cove after high tides and storms. A whale could easily surface beneath me, rolling me off his back. Most of the whales I could hear over a mile away. This particular one I have seen in the cove before, and he is virtually silent. Fortunately this body of water is very quiet, with few motorboats, especially at dawn. Unless it's Darryl's day off and he comes along to watch out for me, I row alone, and am constantly on the alert for that POOOFFF behind me. Harbor seals like to follow me around the cove, frequently bobbing up to look at me when I take a break. They have bumped my boat in the past, so I keep moving when they appear.

Penn Cove is on the east side of Whidbey Island, Washington, USA, in Puget Sound. The cove is the location of the capture of Lolita (Tokitae) in 1970 and numerous other orcas that either died during capture operations or were shipped off to aquariums, where many died young. The resident orcas no longer enter Penn Cove as they remember the tragedies. Only transient, migrating, orcas enter the cove to feed. The harbor seals, food for the orcas, like to gather around the Penn Cove Shellfish farm whose rafts occupy the southwest corner of the cove.

All in all, it is a beautiful place to row. Come join me. No whale encounters guaranteed, but keep your eyes and ears open.

Wendy "Pepper" Schuss

This is the transcript of a video shared with me by San Francisco rowers.[11] It's about a one-person traditional boat called the Whitehall which originated in England around 1500 where it was used by professional wherry men to ship cargo and people across the river Thames in London. Whitehall is a district of London - near where the Houses of Parliament are today and Whitehall Street in New York City is the boatyard where the boats were constructed.

The video ends with a long shot of the side of a boat into which are burned the words *"Renew thyself completely each day, do it again, & again, & forever again."* Which says a lot about the allure of rowing.

The Dolphin Club is a traditional boat rowing club in San Francisco Bay, CA, USA.

Whitehall: The Beauty Of A Wooden Boat

I grew up racing sailboats with my father on the Raritan Bay. He always had a project boat in the yard – an old wooden one that my brother and I would have great seafaring adventures in.

Inside the house, my Dad dreamed his own dreams while he built scale model ships of wood, painstakingly glued and fastened with tiny brass nails.

My first step into the Dolphin Club was a time machine. Here were the life-sized models of my childhood – the detailed woodwork, the metal fastenings, hand-hammered. The lap straight planks, thwarts, gunwales, burden boards sanded then varnished to a high gloss, molded into a functional piece of art.

---

[11] Watch the video: https://youtu.be/gcNhCQMa9eE

The tale of this craft is centuries old. Jon Bielinski, the custodian of this fleet, is like a patient father when he tells me the history of my heart.

"San Francisco was an active, busy port, and these were the sorts of boats that went back and forth, back and forth – you know, taking passengers, taking cargo, going out to ships with pilots and bringing them into the waters. That was the service of the vessel – seaworthy and refined."

"They'd been around 320 years. I mean, it's a long, historical, almost industrial evolution with an aesthetic spin to it, and I liked the way the boats go through the water. I mean, I find the physical exercise restorative. It seems to be something adapted over time to actually work really well with the human body propelling the cargo vessel weight through the water. That's what I like about the boats."

The Whitehall boats are a physical connection to the past – my own – and, when the craft was a workhorse, a trade, until they were replaced with steam engines and ferries. Right around when the sliding seat was born, for racing, for Ivy League rowers.

Jon tells me about the first ones that came here to US about the row boats Sir Francis Drake probably used when he landed here and the migration of it from England to Boston and New York harbours and then westward with the settlers. It always struck me as a bit of romantic history, a beautiful time machine. I think Jon feels some of that, too, he is a steady hand, firm fixture, measuring information, almost mathematically in his way.

"These boats are designed to be built from trees. I need green wood – literally. The sooner it's cut from the tree and put in a steam box and bent to shape, the better. I have been able to locate that and establish relationships with landowners so that their trees can be harvested incrementally and maintaining the aesthetic of the growth wherever it's growing and being sensitive to the needs of the landowner. Usually, they're very generous with the trees that are growing on their property and they're happy to provide it.

Most recently, I've been harvesting wood up in the Sacramento River area where black locust was introduced. I'd gone to Port Townsend to get fine quality, old growth spruce to winnow out one pair of oars at a time, as needed.

The wood is a search, but the result is longevity."

While Jon was completing his master's thesis project – a 35-foot schooner that he lives aboard today – there was a movement to abandon the aging wooden boats and bring in a new fleet of fiberglass ones. Jon arrived at a near-perfect time to begin an era of care and restoration that is a cornerstone of a warm volunteer community which defines Tuesday evenings at the Dolphin Club.

"I sense the historical significance of that effort to maintain this fleet so that the working relationship of these boats and these waters and the occupation that we have here for these boats at the Dolphin Club can continue.

And so, when I put one of them back together – which was the Dino Landucci the first one I repaired – I took the drawing of it. I took the shape of it and then was able to reproduce it, and the reception by the rowers at the Dolphin Club was tremendous. They really were able to compare what was available commercially in fiberglass to what was historically offered in this hull form in wood. It's truly remarkable that Whitehall has survived again and again and again.

There is something to this hull form that engages people, gets them out on the water, brings them back safe, and you don't have to be a collegiate rower. You don't have to be tall or you don't have to be male or anything else to row 'em. They're welcoming."

I think that great societies are made of great communities, and great communities are made of great love. To me, the beauty and effort and warmth of and between the rowboats and its caretakers is a rare and precious thing – a magic gem that each person who touches it takes a piece of it with them forever.

Chris Madell

Chris Madell also gave us this lovely insight into the beauty of boatbuilding and the athlete experience. Silken Laumann is a Canadian three time Olympic medallist in 1984, 1992 and 1996.

Hear This Boat Sing

When I was in Atlanta for the Olympics in 1996, the Canadian Olympic Committee insisted Silken Laumann use a Hudson, rather than the gorgeous wooden Staempfli that had been shipped for her.

It was put up for sale.

A friend of mine who was a bog-awful sculler and who had more money than sense bought it.

She asked me if I'd car-top it from Lake Lanier to Atlanta. I agreed, as long as I was allowed to use it from time to time.

I have this theory that wooden boats sing; this one certainly did.

Printed in Great Britain
by Amazon